Microsoft® Word 6.0
for Windows™
Illustrated Brief Edition

Marie L. Swanson

Course Technology, Inc. One Main Street, Cambridge, MA 02142

An International Thomson Publishing Company

Albany • Bonn • Boston • Cincinnati • London • Madrid • Melbourne • Mexico City
New York • Paris • San Francisco • Singapore • Tokyo • Toronto • Washington

Microsoft Word 6.0 for Windows — Illustrated Brief Edition is published by Course Technology, Inc.

Managing Editor:	Marjorie Hunt
Product Manager:	Nicole Jones Pinard
Production Supervisor:	Kathryn Dinovo
Text Designer:	Leslie Hartwell
Cover Designer:	John Gamache

©1995 Course Technology, Inc.
A Division of International Thomson Publishing, Inc.

For more information contact:
Course Technology, Inc.
One Main Street
Cambridge, MA 02142

International Thomson Publishing Europe
Berkshire House 168-173
High Holborn
London WCIV 7AA
England

International Thomson Publishing GmbH
Königswinterer Strasse 418
53227 Bonn
Germany

Thomas Nelson Australia
102 Dodds Street
South Melbourne, 3205
Victoria, Australia

International Thomson Publishing Asia
211 Henderson Road
#05-10 Henderson Building
Singapore 0315

Nelson Canada
1120 Birchmount Road
Scarborough, Ontario
Canada M1K 5G4

International Thomson Publishing Japan
Hirakawacho Kyowa Building, 3F
2-2-1 Hirakawacho
Chiyoda-ku, Tokyo 102
Japan

International Thomson Editores
Campos Eliseos 385, Piso 7
Col. Polanco
11560 Mexico D.F. Mexico

Trademarks

Course Technology and the open book logo are registered trademarks of Course Technology, Inc.

I(T)P The ITP logo is a trademark under license.

Some of the product names in this book have been used for identification purposes only and may be trademarks or registered trademarks of their respective manufacturers and sellers.

Disclaimer

Course Technology, Inc. reserves the right to revise this publication and make changes from time to time in its content without notice.

ISBN 1-56527-592-6

Printed in the United States of America

10 9 8 7 6 5 4 3

From the Publisher

At Course Technology, Inc., we believe that technology will transform the way that people teach and learn. We are very excited about bringing you, instructors and students, the most practical and affordable technology-related products available.

The Course Technology Development Process

Our development process is unparalleled in the educational publishing industry. Every product we create goes through an exacting process of design, development, review, and testing.

Reviewers give us direction and insight that shape our manuscripts and bring them up to the latest standards. Every manuscript is quality tested. Students whose background matches the intended audience work through every keystroke, carefully checking for clarity and pointing out errors in logic and sequence. Together with our technical reviewers, these testers help us ensure that everything that carries our name is as error free and easy to use as possible.

Course Technology Products

We show both *how* and *why* technology is critical to solving problems in the classroom and in whatever field you choose to teach or pursue. Our time-tested, step-by-step instructions provide unparalleled clarity. Examples and applications are chosen and crafted to motivate students.

The Course Technology Team

This book will suit your needs because it was delivered quickly, efficiently, and affordably. In every aspect of business, we rely on a commitment to quality and the use of technology. Every employee contributes to this process. The names of all our employees are listed below: Tim Ashe, David Backer, Stephen M. Bayle, Josh Bernoff, Ann Marie Buconjic, Jody Buttafoco, Kerry Cannell, Jim Chrysikos, Barbara Clemens, Amy Clemons, Susan Collins, John M. Connolly, Kim Crowley, Myrna D'Addario, Lisa D'Alessandro, Jodi Davis, Howard S. Diamond, Kathryn Dinovo, Joseph B. Dougherty, Laurie Duncan, Karen Dwyer, MaryJane Dwyer, Kristin Dyer, Chris Elkhill, Don Fabricant, Viktor Frengut, Jeff Goding, Laurie Gomes, Eileen Gorham, Catherine Griffin, Tim Hale, Jamie Harper, Roslyn Hooley, John Hope, Marjorie Hunt, Matt Kenslea, Susannah Lean, Kim Mai, Margaret Makowski, Tammy Marciano, Elizabeth Martinez, Debbie Masi, Don Maynard, Dan Mayo, Kathleen McCann, Sarah McLean, Jay McNamara, Mac Mendelsohn, Karla Mitchell, Kim Munsell, Amy Oliver, Michael Ormsby, Debbie Parlee, Kristin Patrick, Charlie Patsios, Darren Perl, Kevin Phaneuf, George J. Pilla, Nicole Jones Pinard, Cathy Prindle, Nancy Ray, Laura Sacks, Carla Sharpe, Deborah Shute, Jennifer Slivinski, Christine Spillett, Michelle Tucker, David Upton, Mark Valentine, Karen Wadsworth, Renee Walkup, Tracy Wells, Donna Whiting, Janet Wilson, Lisa Yameen.

Preface

Course Technology, Inc. is proud to present this new book in its Illustrated Series. *Microsoft Word 6.0 for Windows — Illustrated Brief Edition* provides a highly visual, hands-on introduction to Microsoft Word. The book is designed as a learning tool for Word novices but will also be useful as a source for future reference. It assumes students have learned basic Windows skills and file management from *Microsoft Windows 3.1 — Illustrated Brief Edition* or from an equivalent book.

Organization and Coverage

Microsoft Word 6.0 for Windows — Illustrated Brief Edition contains four units that cover basic Word skills. In these units students learn how to plan, build, edit, and enhance documents. The book also covers creating tables, inserting graphics, and using styles.

Approach

Microsoft Word 6.0 for Windows — Illustrated Brief Edition distinguishes itself from other textbooks with its highly visual approach to computer instruction.

Lessons: Information Displays

The basic lesson format of this text is the "information display," a two-page lesson that is sharply focused on a specific task. This sharp focus and the precise beginning and end of a lesson make it easy for students to study specific material. Modular lessons are less overwhelming for students, and they provide instructors with more flexibility in planning classes and assigning specific work. The units are modular as well and can be presented in any order.

Each lesson, or "information display," contains the following elements:

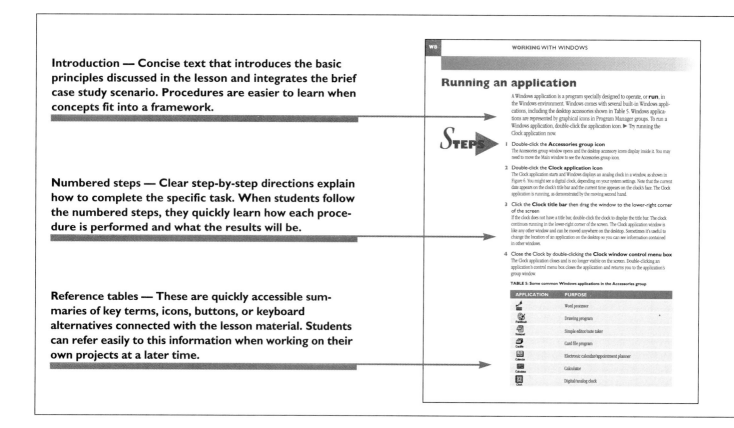

Introduction — Concise text that introduces the basic principles discussed in the lesson and integrates the brief case study scenario. Procedures are easier to learn when concepts fit into a framework.

Numbered steps — Clear step-by-step directions explain how to complete the specific task. When students follow the numbered steps, they quickly learn how each procedure is performed and what the results will be.

Reference tables — These are quickly accessible summaries of key terms, icons, buttons, or keyboard alternatives connected with the lesson material. Students can refer easily to this information when working on their own projects at a later time.

Features

Microsoft Word 6.0 for Windows — Illustrated Brief Edition is an exceptional textbook because it contains the following features:

- "Read This Before You Begin Microsoft Word 6.0" Page — This page provides essential information that both students and instructors need to know before they begin working through the units.

- Real-World Case — The case study used throughout the textbook is designed to be "real-world" in nature and representative of the kinds of activities that students will encounter when working with word processing software. With a real-world case, the process of learning skills will be more meaningful to students.

- End of Unit Material — Each unit concludes with a meaningful Concepts Review that tests students' understanding of what they learned in the unit. The Concepts Review is followed by an Applications Review, which provides students with additional hands-on practice of the skills they learned in the unit. The Applications Review is followed by Independent Challenges, which pose case problems for students to solve. The Independent Challenges allow students to learn by exploring and develop critical thinking skills.

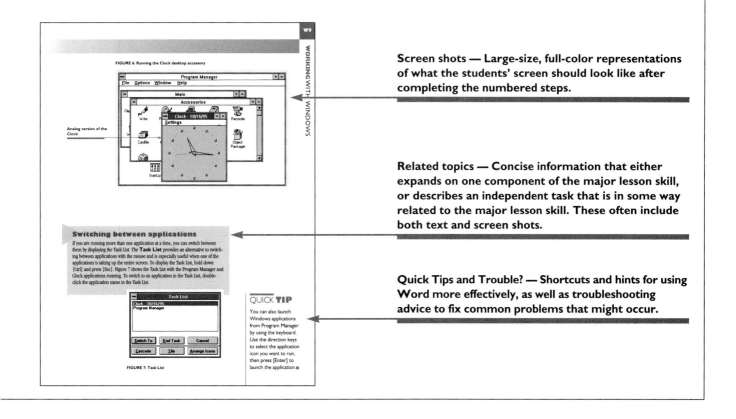

Screen shots — Large-size, full-color representations of what the students' screen should look like after completing the numbered steps.

Related topics — Concise information that either expands on one component of the major lesson skill, or describes an independent task that is in some way related to the major lesson skill. These often include both text and screen shots.

Quick Tips and Trouble? — Shortcuts and hints for using Word more effectively, as well as troubleshooting advice to fix common problems that might occur.

The Student Disk

The Student Disk bundled with the instructor's copy of this book contains all the data files students need to complete the step-by-step lessons.

Adopters of this text are granted the right to post the Student Disk on any standalone computer or network used by students who have purchased this product.

For more information on the Student Disk, see the page in this book called "Read This Before You Begin Microsoft Word 6.0."

The Supplements

Instructor's Manual — The Instructor's Manual is quality assurance tested. It includes:

- Solutions to all lessons, Concept Reviews, Application Reviews, and Independent Challenges
- A disk containing solutions to all of the lessons, Concept Reviews, Application Reviews, and Independent Challenges
- Unit notes, which contain tips from the author about the instructional progression of each lesson
- Extra problems
- Transparency masters of key concepts

Test Bank — The Test Bank contains approximately 50 questions per unit in true/false, multiple choice, and fill-in-the-blank formats, plus two essay questions. Each question has been quality assurance tested by students to achieve clarity and accuracy.

Electronic Test Bank — The Electronic Test Bank allows instructors to edit individual test questions, select questions individually or at random, and print out scrambled versions of the same test to any supported printer.

Acknowledgments

This book is the product of the labors of many patient, energetic, and supportive people. My editorial assistant, Shari Dornquast, deserves special thanks for her careful proofreading, keystroking, picture-taking, and moral support. For her infinite patience and guidance regarding instructional motivation, many thanks go to Kathy Finnegan, my developmental editor. Other Course Technology staffers kept the process moving smoothly: the student reviewers ensured that the step-by-step instructions worked as expected, Kathryn Dinovo, the production supervisor, coordinated the production of the final package with skill and persistence, and Nicole Jones Pinard, as product manager, kept everyone in good spirits so we could meet her deadlines and deliver a great book.

Marie L. Swanson

Contents

UNIT 4 — Arranging Text and Graphics

TABLES

Microsoft Word 6.0

for Windows™

Read This Before You Begin
Microsoft Word 6.0

Word 6.0 Screen Check

At the beginning of each unit, verify that:
- The document window is maximized, and the document is displayed in Normal View.
- Only the Standard and Formatting toolbars are displayed.
- The scroll bars and the ruler are displayed.
- The Show/Hide button is selected, and magnification is set to 100%.
- The default font is Times New Roman, and the default point size is 10.

To the Student

The exercises and examples in this book feature sample Word document files stored on the Student Disk provided to your instructor. To complete the step-by-step exercises in this book, you must have a Student Disk. Your instructor will either provide you with your own copy of the Student Disk or will make the Student Disk files available to you over a network in your school's computer lab. See your instructor or technical support person for further information.

Using Your Own Computer

If you are going to work through this book using your own computer, you need a computer system running Microsoft Windows 3.1, Microsoft Word 6.0 for Windows, and a Student Disk. *You will not be able to complete the step-by-step exercises in this book using your own computer until you have your own Student Disk.* This book assumes the default settings under a Complete installation of Microsoft Word 6.0 for Windows. Do not install "Help for WordPerfect users."

To the Instructor

Bundled with the instructor's copy of this book is the Student Disk, which contains all the files your students need to complete the step-by-step exercises in this book. Adopters of this text are granted the right to distribute the files on the Student Disk to any student who has purchased a copy of this text. You are free to post all of these files to a network or standalone workstations, or simply provide copies of the disk to your students. The instructions in this book assume that the students know which drive and directory contain the Student Disk files, so it's important that you provide disk location information before the students start working through the units. This book also assumes that Word 6.0 is set up using the Complete installation procedure.

Using the Student Disk Files

To keep the original files on the Student Disk intact, the instructions in this book for opening files require two important steps: (1) open the existing file and (2) save it as a new file with a new name. This procedure ensures that the original file will remain unmodified in case the student wants to redo the exercise.

To organize their files, students are instructed to save their files to the MY_FILES directory on their Student Disk that they created in *Microsoft Windows 3.1*. In case your students did not complete this lesson, it is included in the Instructor's Manual that accompanies this book. You can circulate this to your students, or you can instruct them to simply save to drive A or drive B.

UNIT 1

Getting Started
WITH MICROSOFT
WORD 6.0

fter learning the basics of using Microsoft Windows, you have the skills
you need to learn how to use Microsoft Word 6.0 for Windows. The
lessons in this unit introduce you to the basic features of Word and famil-
iarize you with the Word environment so that you can use Word effectively. ▶ Angela Pacheco is the marketing manager at Nomad Ltd, an
outdoor sporting gear and adventure travel company. Angela's responsibilities include communicating with new and current customers about
the company. To make her job easier, she'll be using Word to create
attractive and professional-looking documents for both internal communications and correspondence to customers. She'll begin by exploring the
Word environment. ▶

Defining word processing software

Microsoft Word 6.0 is a full-featured **word processing** application that allows you to create attractive and professional-looking documents quickly and easily. Word processing offers many advantages compared to typing. Because the information you enter in a word processing document is stored electronically by your computer, it is easy to revise and reuse text in documents you have already created. In addition, you can enhance your documents by giving text a special appearance and adding lines, shading, and even pictures (called **graphics**). Figure 1-1 illustrates the kinds of features you can use in your documents.

With word processing software, Angela will be able to perform the following tasks:

■ **Locate and correct spelling mistakes and grammatical errors**
After Angela and her colleagues in the Marketing Department use Word to create documents for the Annual Report, they use Word's proofreading tools to identify errors and correct them.

■ **Copy and move text and graphics without retyping**
Angela can save time by copying text found in other documents, and using it again in the material for the Annual Report. Within the same document, she can reorganize text and graphics.

■ **Enhance the appearance of documents by adding formatting**
By applying different types of formatting to important parts of documents, Angela can create documents that convey their message quickly and effectively to their readers. Word features, such as the Formatting toolbar and AutoFormat, help Angela do this quickly.

■ **Align text in rows and columns using tables**
Although Nomad uses a spreadsheet application, Microsoft Excel, for complex financial analysis, Angela can use tables in Word to present small amounts of financial information in an easy-to-read format.

■ **Add visual interest to documents by inserting graphics and arranging text in different ways**
Before using Word, Angela often used expensive desktop publishing resources outside the company to create attractive and professional-looking newsletters and other marketing materials. Now she can use Word to create the professional documents she needs, without the extra cost.

■ **Preview a document as it will look when printed**
Before printing her documents, Angela can preview all the pages of her work at one time. By getting the "big picture" of the document, she can catch mistakes and make final adjustments before printing.

FIGURE I-I: Features in a Word document

Header → Volume 1, Issue 1

Bold and italics text

Border

Nomad Ltd
Executive Bulletin

Table

Text formatted in columns

Division	FY 1994	FY 1993	FY 1992	Total
Northeast	800	700	600	2100
West	1000	900	600	2500
Southwest	800	600	500	1900
Northwest	625	400	300	1325
Nomad Ltd	3225	2600	2000	7825

Balancing the Books

This year's sales continued the trend of rising revenues. For the second consecutive year, we exceeded the goals set forth in the President's Plan. We also implemented many new cost saving measures, many of which were suggested during employee retreats and brainstorming weekends.

The combination of increased sales revenue, especially in the northeast markets, and the innovative cost cutting measures was recognized and well-received by the Wall Street establishment and the financial press. We are also pleased to report that Nomad Ltd is a profitable component in the portfolios of all major "green" mutual funds.

Framed and positioned text

Milestones

Bulleted list

- Achieved 163% of plan for the year, a new record!
- Introduced South American adventures in New Directions™ travel division.
- Increased Northeast sales 65%.

Shaded text

Inserted graphics

Communications

Developed in-house publishing department to produce all corporate communications including the annual report, the corporate newsletter, and corporate catalogs. Completed year-long search for new director of communications.

Quality Assurance

Formalized and implemented Product Testing and Standards review process. Installed Product Testing Center. Began working with guiding and outdoor leadership organizations to field test all products including outer wear and recreational gear.

New Directions™ Travel

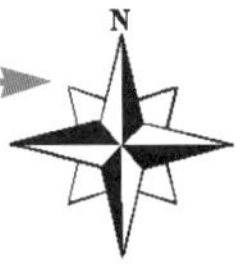

Purchased two national guiding services and another with international connections. Combined, these organizations will deliver services through the New Directions subsidiary. This diversification will allow Nomad Ltd to offer new tours in exciting locations, including South America and Africa.

Environmental Relations

Established Environmental Relations department to focus on both internal environmental awareness and education, as well as researching recyclable products. This department will also work with the travel division to explore the future of eco-tourism.

Corporate Mission Statement

Drop cap → Nomad Ltd is a national sporting-goods retailer dedicated to delivering high-quality adventure sporting gear and clothing.

Footer → ©1995, Nomad Ltd

Starting Word 6.0 for Windows

To start Word, you first start Windows, as described in "Microsoft Windows 3.1." Then, you open the program group window that contains the Word application icon—usually the Microsoft Office program group. If you are using a computer on a network, your procedure for starting Word might be different. Ask your technical support person or instructor if there are any special procedures for starting Word on your computer. ▶ Angela's first step in learning to use Word is to start the application.

1 Make sure the Program Manager window is open
The Program Manager icon might appear at the bottom of your screen. Double-click it to open it, if necessary.

2 Double-click the **Microsoft Office program group icon**
The Microsoft Word icon appears inside the Microsoft Office program group, as shown in Figure 1-2. Depending on the applications installed on your computer, the icons shown in this program group might be different. If you cannot locate the Microsoft Office program group, click Window on the Program Manager menu bar, then click Microsoft Office.

3 Double-click the **Microsoft Word application icon**
Word opens and displays the Tip of the Day dialog box, which provides a brief note describing a Word feature or command. (If the Tip of the Day dialog box does not open, this feature has been **disabled** (turned off) by someone else using the computer you're working on; skip Step 4 and continue with the next lesson.) Later in this unit, you will learn about dialog boxes. For now, you'll simply close the dialog box.

4 Click **OK**
The Tip of the Day dialog box closes, and the application window appears, as shown in Figure 1-3. The blinking vertical line, called the **insertion point**, in the application window indicates where text will appear when you begin typing. When you first start the Word application, you can begin creating a new document right away. You will learn how to type in a new document in the next unit. For now Angela continues to explore basic Word features.

FIGURE I-2: Microsoft Office program group

Microsoft Word application icon

Your available applications might vary

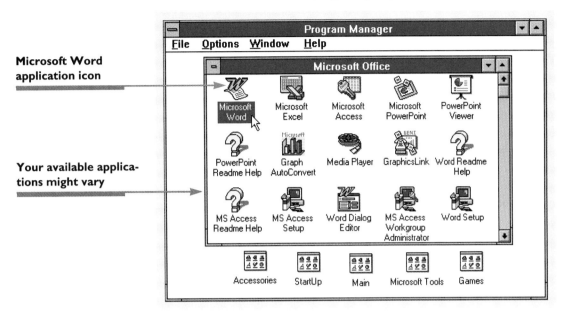

FIGURE I-3: Word application window

Insertion point

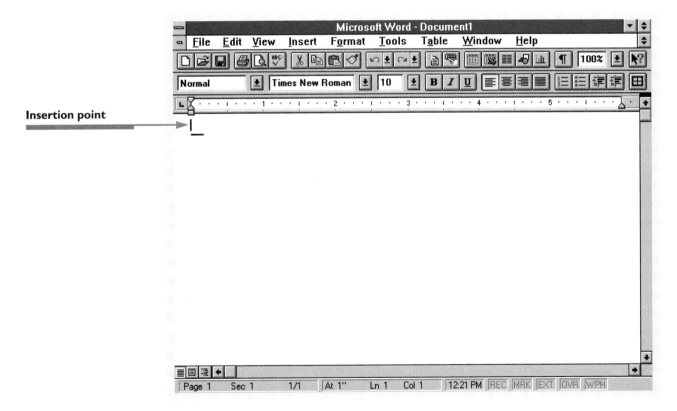

Viewing the Word application window

The Word **application window** contains the features described below. On your computer, locate each of the elements using Figure 1-4 for reference.

■ The **title bar** displays the name of the application and the document. Until you save the document and give it a name, the temporary name for the document is DOCUMENT1.

■ The **menu bar** lists the names of the menus that contain Word commands. Clicking a menu name on the menu bar displays a list of commands from which you can choose.

■ The **Standard toolbar** contains buttons for the most frequently used commands, such as the commands for opening, saving, and printing documents. Clicking buttons on a toolbar is often faster than using the menu. However, in some cases, using the menu offers additional options not available by clicking a button. You can find out what a button does by displaying its ToolTip. See the related topic "ToolTips" for more information. This toolbar is one of the two default toolbars.

■ The **Formatting toolbar** contains buttons for the most frequently used formatting commands, such as the commands for applying bold to text or aligning text. This toolbar is one of the two default toolbars. Other toolbars related to other features are also available, as you will see in later units.

■ The **horizontal ruler** displays tab settings, left and right paragraph and document margins, and column widths (only in page layout view). In page layout view, a **vertical ruler** is also displayed. You'll learn more about the different Word views later in this book.

■ The **document window** displays the work area for typing text and working with your document. When the mouse pointer is in the document window, the pointer changes to an **I-beam**, I. You can have as many document windows open as you want. Each window can be minimized, maximized, and sized. When you are working in only one document at a time, it is a good idea to maximize the document window.

■ The **vertical and horizontal scroll bars** display the relative position of the currently displayed text in the document. You use the scroll bars and scroll boxes to view different parts of your document.

■ The **view buttons**, which appear in the horizontal scroll bar, allow you to display the document in one of three views. Each view offers features that are useful in the different phases of working with a document. You'll learn more about the three views later in this book.

■ The **status bar** displays the current page number and section number, the total number of pages in the document, and the vertical position of the insertion point (in inches and in lines from the upper-left corner of the document). You also see the status of commands in effect and the current time. The status bar also displays descriptions of commands and buttons as you move around the window.

FIGURE I-4: Elements of the Word application window

Title bar

Menu bar

Standard toolbar

Formatting toolbar

Horizontal ruler

Document window

Scroll box

Scroll bars

Scroll box

View buttons

Status bar

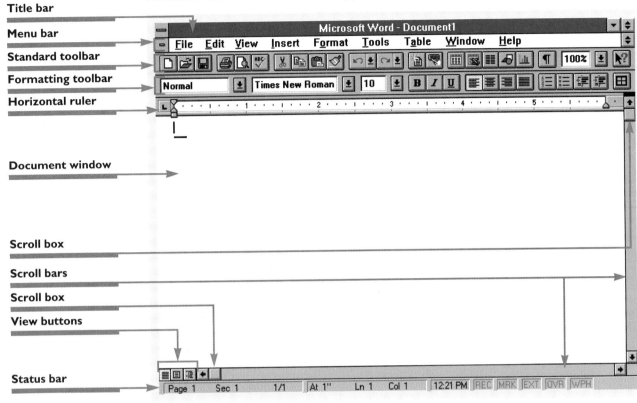

ToolTips

As you move the mouse pointer over a button on a toolbar, the name of the button—called a **ToolTip**—appears below or above the button. A brief description of the button also appears in the status bar.

TROUBLE?

If your document window is not maximized, click the document window Maximize button. If the Page Layout View button 🔲 in the horizontal scroll bar appears "depressed," indicating it is selected, the document is in page layout view. To display the document in normal view, click the Normal View button 🔲 in the horizontal scroll bar.∎

Working with dialog boxes, toolbars, and buttons

Word often provides several ways to complete the same task—using menus, toolbars, or keyboard shortcuts. After you become familiar with the different techniques, use the one you prefer. Before you can begin using Word to create and edit documents, you need to become familiar with using dialog boxes, toolbars, and buttons to perform tasks. ▶ Angela decides to turn off the option for displaying the Tip of the Day dialog box when she starts Word and to display special characters that represent how text is formatted.

1 Click Help on the menu bar, then click Tip of the Day
The Tip of the Day dialog box opens, as shown in Figure 1-5. Note that the text in your dialog box might be different. Clicking a command that has an ellipsis (...) displays a dialog box in which you can specify the options you want for the command. In the Tip of the Day dialog box, you can view helpful hints for using Word, and specify whether this dialog box opens when you start Word. The "x" in the Show Tips at Startup check box indicates that the feature is activated. If the check box on your screen does not contain an "x," click OK and skip to Step 3.

2 Click the Show Tips at Startup check box to remove the "x," then click OK or press [Enter]
Clearing this check box disables the Show Tips at Startup option so that this dialog box will not open automatically when you start Word. You can click OK or press [Enter] to carry out a command; otherwise, click Cancel or press [Esc] to close a dialog box without making a change.

3 Click the Show/Hide ¶ button ¶ on the Standard toolbar, as shown in Figure 1-6
This button displays nonprinting characters that represent spaces, paragraphs, and tabs, as shown in Table 1-1. Displaying these characters helps you recognize the format of a document as you work in it. These characters appear only on the screen, not in your printed documents. Note that when you click ¶, it appears "depressed," indicating it is selected. If you click the button again, the nonprinting characters are not displayed. In this book, you will usually work with nonprinting characters displayed.

Figure 1-6 also identifies buttons you will use later in this unit.

TABLE 1-1: Nonprinting characters

NONPRINTING CHARACTER	REPRESENTS
¶	Paragraph mark
.	Space
→	Tab character

FIGURE I-5: Tip of the Day dialog box

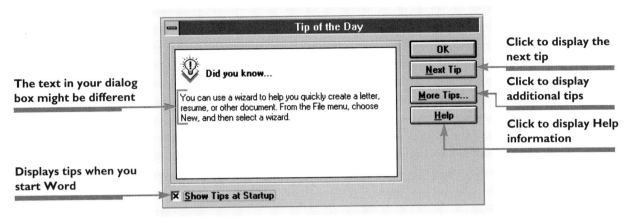

The text in your dialog box might be different

Displays tips when you start Word

Click to display the next tip

Click to display additional tips

Click to display Help information

FIGURE I-6: Standard and Formatting toolbars

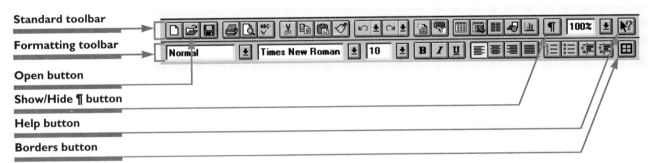

Standard toolbar

Formatting toolbar

Open button

Show/Hide ¶ button

Help button

Borders button

TROUBLE?

The Standard and Formatting toolbars appear by default in the Word application window. If you cannot see the Standard or Formatting toolbar, click View on the menu bar then click Toolbars. In the Toolbars dialog box, you can click the check boxes for the toolbars you want to display. Verify that only the Standard and Formatting check boxes are checked.■

Working with dialog boxes, toolbars, and buttons, continued

In addition to the menus on the menu bar, Word has shortcut menus. These offer another method for performing tasks quickly. See the related topic "Using shortcut menus" for more information. ▶ Angela wants to explore the Word environment further by viewing another toolbar and dialog box.

4 **Click the Borders button** ▦ **on the Formatting toolbar**
Clicking this button displays the Borders toolbar below the Formatting toolbar. Later in this book, you will learn to use the Borders toolbar to add lines and shading to text.

5 **Click** ▦ **again**
The Borders button is no longer selected, and the Borders toolbar is no longer displayed. Next, Angela wants to view the features available on the Options dialog box.

6 **Click Tools on the menu bar, then click Options**
The Options dialog box opens, as shown in Figure 1-7. Note that the dialog box is divided into **tabs**, or different sections. Each tab in this dialog box contains options you can specify for different Word features. For example, you can choose to display only some of the nonprinting characters when you click the Show/Hide ¶ button. However, Angela wants to be sure that *all* of the nonprinting characters appear when she clicks this button.

7 **Click the View tab (if it is not already the frontmost tab) and make sure the All check box in the Nonprinting Characters section is checked**
If the All check box does not contain an "x," click the check box. You can display and choose options for other Word features by clicking the appropriate tab. For now, Angela closes the dialog box, so she can continue exploring Word.

8 **Click Cancel to close the dialog box (or click OK if you selected the All option in Step 7)**

FIGURE 1-7: Options dialog box

Click tabs to display options for specific features

Check boxes for specific options

Specifies that all nonprinting characters appear in document window

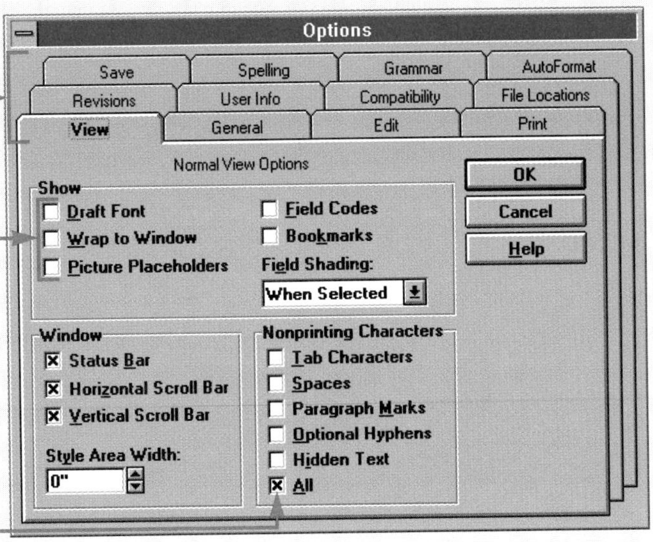

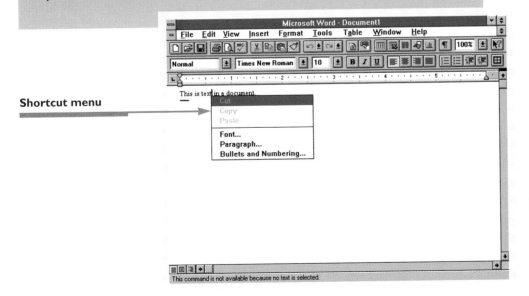

Using shortcut menus

Shortcut menus contain commands you are likely to use in specific situations. You display a shortcut menu by clicking the right mouse button. For example, when you click text with the right mouse button, you see a menu of commands that are useful when editing text, as shown in Figure 1-8. You close a shortcut menu by clicking anywhere outside the menu.

Shortcut menu

FIGURE 1-8: Shortcut menu in the document window

TROUBLE?

If you choose a command by mistake, click Edit on the menu bar, then click Undo. The Undo command reverses the results of your last action.■

Opening a document and moving through it

To view or work in a Word document, you first need to open the document. You can use either the Open command on the File menu or the Open button on the Standard toolbar to open a document. ▶ Angela wants to view a document created by one of her colleagues in the Marketing Department.

I Place your Student Disk in drive A

To complete the units in this book, you need a Student Disk. See your instructor for a copy of the Student Disk, if you do not already have one. Also, these lessons assume your Student Disk is in drive A. If you are using a different drive or if your practice files are stored on a network, ask your technical support person or instructor where to find your practice files.

2 Click the **Open button** 📂 on the Standard toolbar

Word displays the Open dialog box, as shown in Figure 1-9. In this dialog box, you select the document you want to open. The files, directories, and drive names on your computer might be different from those shown in the figure.

3 Click the **Drives list arrow**, then click **a:**

The list of files stored on drive A appears in the File Name list box. In this case, the list shows the documents you will use to learn about Word.

4 In the File Name list box, click **UNIT_I-I.DOC**, then click **OK**

The document UNIT_1-1.DOC opens in the document window. Table 1-2 describes the different ways in which you can move around in a document. To review the document, Angela uses a variety of techniques to display different parts of the document.

5 Click the **down scroll arrow** at the bottom of the vertical scroll bar, then click the **up scroll arrow** at the top of the vertical scroll bar

When you click the down scroll arrow, the first line in the document scrolls off the top of the screen and a new line of text appears at the bottom. When you click the up scroll arrow, the window scrolls up one line.

6 Click below the scroll box in the vertical scroll bar, then click above the scroll box

The window scrolls down then up one window of text. When you use the scroll arrows and bars to move around in a document, you are simply displaying other parts of the document; the insertion point does *not* move. To move the insertion point, you must either click the left mouse button at the location you want, or use one of the techniques described in Table 1-2.

7 Drag the scroll box to the bottom of the vertical scroll bar, then click the **left mouse button** to place the insertion point at the end of the document

8 Press and hold **[Ctrl]** and press **[Home]**

The first part of the document appears in the document window, and the insertion point is located in front of the first character in the document.

If a dialog box opens when you press [Ctrl][Home], the Help for WordPerfect Users option has been activated on your computer. You need to deactivate this option so that the navigation keys will work as noted in this book. To turn the option off, double-click WPH in the status bar, click Options to display the Help Options dialog box, clear the Help for WordPerfect Users check box and the Navigation Keys for WordPerfect Users check box, click OK, then click Close.

FIGURE I-9:
Open dialog box

Selected file to open appears here

Filenames in current directory appear in list

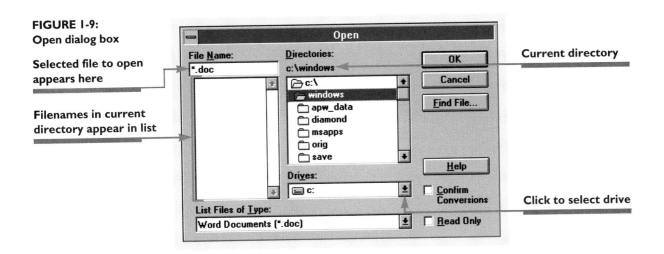

Current directory

Click to select drive

TABLE I-2: Keyboard navigation techniques

TO MOVE	PRESS
Left one character	The Left Arrow key [←]
Right one character	The Right Arrow key [→]
Left one word	[Ctrl][←]
Right one word	[Ctrl][→]
To the start of a line	[Home]
To the end of a line	[End]
Up one line	The Up Arrow key [↑]
Down one line	The Down Arrow key [↓]
Up one paragraph	[Ctrl][↑]
Down one paragraph	[Ctrl][↓]
Up one screen	[Page Up]
Down one screen	[Page Down]
To the first character on the first page	[Ctrl][Home]
To the last character on the last page	[Ctrl][End]

QUICK **TIP**

To go to a specific page in a document, double-click the page number in the status bar. In the Go To dialog box, type the number of the page you want to go to, then press [Enter].■

TROUBLE?

The [Home], [End], [Page Up], and [Page Down] keys are located above the arrow keys on your keyboard.■

Getting Help

The Word application includes an on-line Help system that provides information and instructions on Word features and commands while you are using Word. You can get as little or as much information as you want, from quick definitions to detailed procedures. See the related topic "More about using Help" for additional information. Table 1-3 describes the Help commands available on the Help menu. You can also get help by clicking the Help button that is available in most dialog boxes. ▶ In her role as marketing manager for Nomad Ltd, Angela expects to create documents that contain many pages. She decides to use Word's on-line Help to learn how to move quickly to a specific page.

1 Click **Help** on the menu bar
The Help menu displays the Help commands, which are described in Table 1-3.

2 Click **Search for Help on**
The Search dialog box opens, as shown in Figure 1-10. In this dialog box, you can type a topic and view the entries that provide more information. Notice that the insertion point is in the search text box, ready for you to type the topic for which you want to search. Angela wants more information on navigating through a document.

3 In the search text box, type **navigating** then click **Show Topics**
Notice that as you type each character, topics that match your typing appear in the search topics list. After you click Show Topics, a list of related topics appears in the bottom of the Search dialog box. Next, Angela selects the specific topic that will provide the information she needs.

4 Click the text **Going to a page, bookmark, footnote, table, annotation, graphic,** (if it is not already selected), then click **Go To**
Information about moving around in a document appears in the How To window. Read this information to learn more about moving to a specific location in a document.

5 Scroll the How To window, then click the underlined text **Go To command**
The Help window displays information about the Go To command. Clicking underlined text displays a Help window about the underlined topic. You can return to the previous topic by clicking Back. Angela wants to clarify her understanding of the insertion point.

6 Click the dotted underlined text **insertion point**
A pop-up window defining the insertion point appears. Clicking text underlined with a dotted line displays a definition.

7 Read the information then click anywhere in the pop-up window to close it

8 Double-click the **control menu box** on the current Help window to close it
The Help window about the Go To command closes, but the How To window remains open.

9 Double-click the **control menu box** on the How To window to close it
The How To window closes, and you return to the document.

FIGURE 1-10: Search dialog box

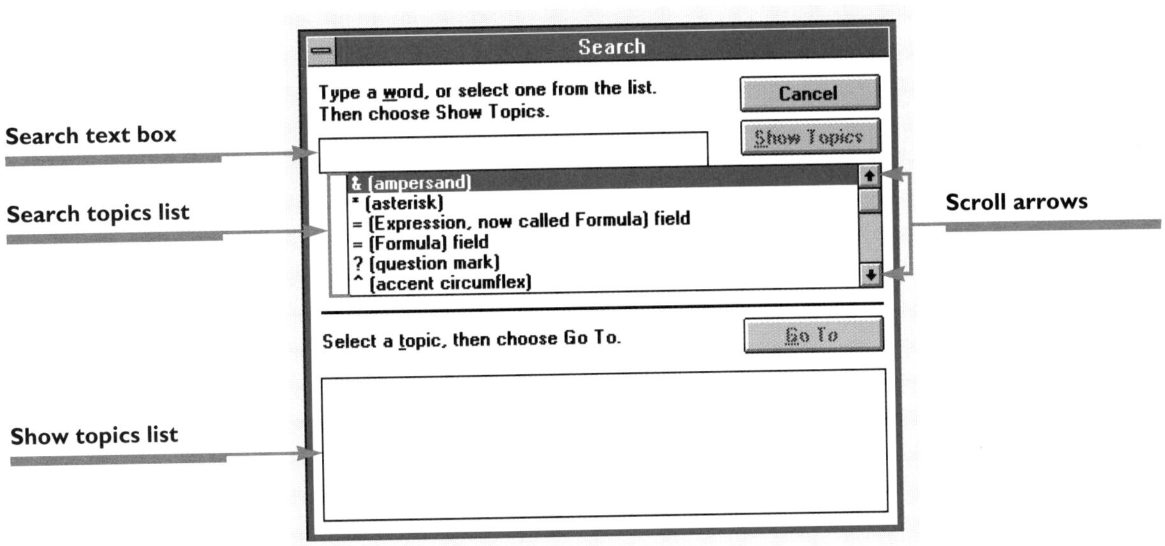

Search text box

Search topics list

Show topics list

Scroll arrows

More about using Help

By clicking Contents on the Help menu, then clicking Using Word, you can display general word processing categories. By clicking the underlined text, you can jump to a specific topic. You can move and size the Help window if it blocks your view of the document. To work in the document and display the Help window at the same time, choose Always on Top from the Help menu in the Word Help window.

TABLE 1-3: Help commands

HELP COMMAND	DESCRIPTION
Contents	Displays Help topic categories
Search for Help on	Displays Search dialog box in which you can search for a specific topic
Index	Displays alphabetical list of Help topics
Quick Preview	Displays demonstrations about Getting Started, What's New?, Tips for WordPerfect Users
Examples and Demos	Displays a demonstration of a selected Word feature
Tip of the Day	Displays Tip of the Day dialog box for viewing helpful hints
WordPerfect Help	Shows the Word equivalent for a WordPerfect command
Technical Support	Displays information about support services
About Microsoft Word	Displays licensing and system information

QUICK **TIP**

Use the Help pointer �? to get Help information about any part of the window. Click the Help button ▣ on the Standard toolbar, then with the Help pointer click an item to display information about it.■

Closing a document and exiting Word

After you have finished working in a document, you generally save your work and then close the document. When you are done using Word, you need to exit the application. For a comparison of the Close and Exit commands, refer to Table 1-4. ▶ Angela has finished exploring the Word document for now, so she closes the document and exits the application.

I   Click **File** on the menu bar, then click **Close**
When you close a document after making changes that you have not saved, Word asks whether you want to save your changes. You also see this same message when you exit the application before saving changes in the document. Because Angela did not make any changes to the document (she was just reviewing it to explore Word features and to see what her colleague had written), she will close the document without saving it.

2   If the message appears asking if you want to save changes, click **No**
The document closes, and Word displays the application window with only the File and Help menus available, as shown in Figure 1-11.

3   Click **File** on the menu bar, then click **Exit**
The Exit command closes the Word application and returns you to the Program Manager.

TABLE I-4: Close vs. Exit

CLOSING A DOCUMENT	EXITING WORD
Puts away the document file	Puts away all files
Leaves Word running so that you can choose to open another document or use on-line Help	Returns you to the Program Manager where you can choose to run another application

FIGURE 1-11: Word window with no open documents

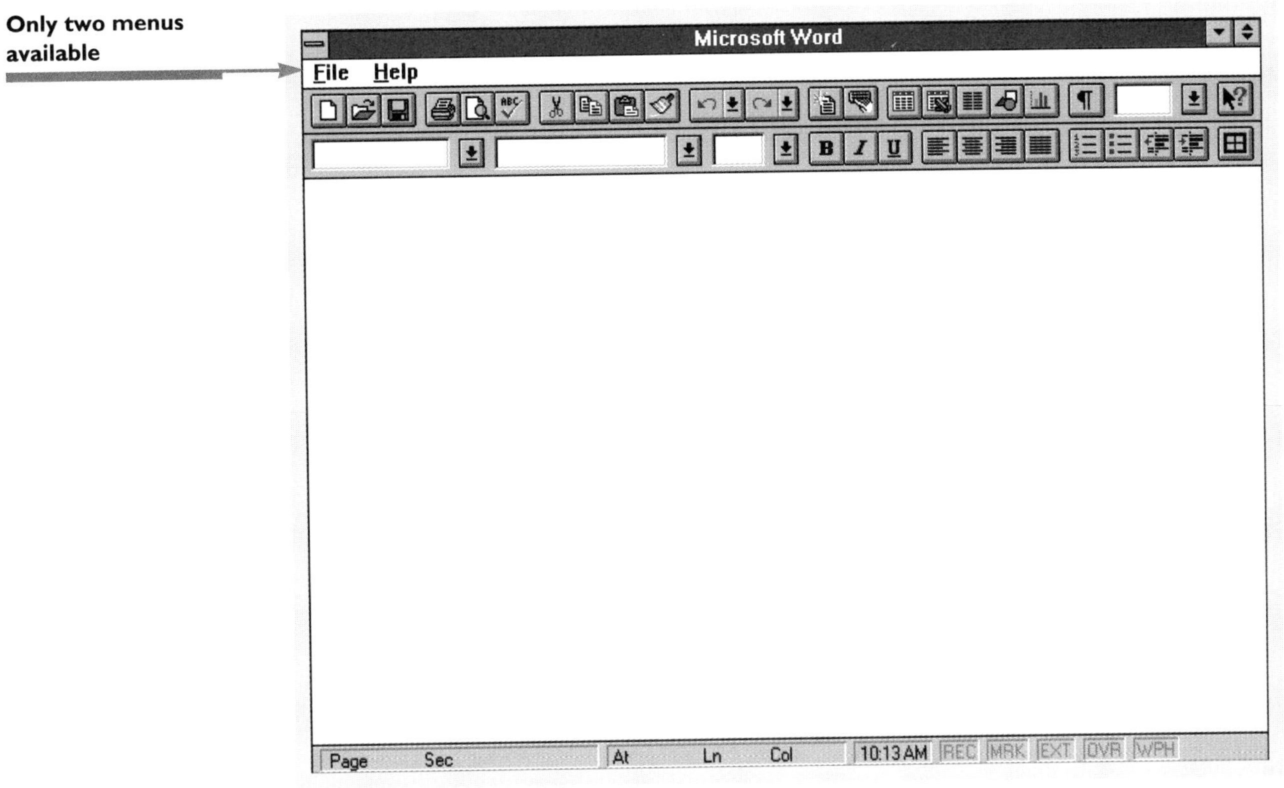

Only two menus available

QUICK **TIP**

Double-clicking the control menu box next to the menu bar closes the document. Double-clicking the control menu box in the title bar exits the application.■

CONCEPTSREVIEW

Label each of the elements of the Word application window in Figure 1-12.

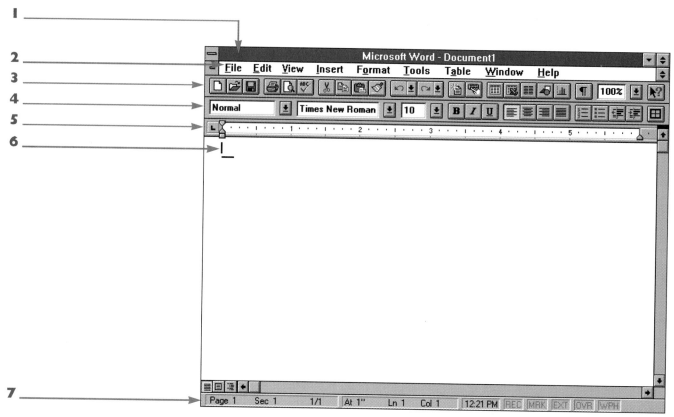

FIGURE 1-12

Match each of the following terms with the statement that best describes its function.

8 Toolbar

9 Document window

10 Ruler

11 Status bar

12 Right mouse button

    a. Displays area in which you enter text

    b. Identifies location of insertion point, command status, button descriptions

    c. Contains buttons for easy access to commands

    d. Displays shortcut menus

    e. Displays tab settings, paragraph and document margins, and column width

Select the best answer from the list of choices.

13 Word processing is similar to

    a. Performing financial analysis

    b. Filling in forms

    c. Typing

    d. Forecasting mortgage payments

14 To display another part of a document, you

    a. Click in the Moving toolbar

    b. Scroll with a scroll bar

    c. Drag the ruler

    d. Select the control menu box

15 Commands followed by an ellipsis (...)

    a. Are unavailable

    b. Are available on the Formatting toolbar

    c. Display Help information when you choose them

    d. Display a dialog box when you choose them

16 You can get Help in any of the following ways, EXCEPT:

    a. Clicking Help in a dialog box

    b. Double-clicking anywhere in the document window

    c. Clicking the Help button on the Standard toolbar

    d. Clicking Help on the menu bar

17 To search for a topic in Help, you

    a. Click Help on the menu bar, then click Search for Help on

    b. Select the command then click the Help button on the Standard toolbar

    c. Click the Help button on the Standard toolbar

    d. Click the Help button on the Formatting toolbar

18 The Close command on the File menu

    a. Closes Word without saving any changes

    b. Closes the current document and, if you have made any changes, asks if you want to save them

    c. Closes all currently open Word documents

    d. Closes the current document without saving changes

APPLICATIONSREVIEW

1 Start Word then identify the parts of the window.

    a. Double-click the Microsoft Office program group icon in the Program Manager window.

    b. Double-click the Microsoft Word application icon.

    c. Read the Tip of the Day, if it appears. Clear the Show Tips at Startup check box, then click OK.

    d. Identify as many elements of the Word window as you can without referring to the unit material.

2 Explore the Word document window.

    a. Click each of the menus and drag the mouse button through all the commands on each menu. Read the command descriptions that appear in the status bar. To close a menu without making a selection, drag the mouse away from the menu, then release the mouse button.

    b. Point to each of the buttons on the toolbars, and read the ToolTips and descriptions.

    c. Click Tools then click Options. In the Options dialog box, click the Edit tab and make sure that the first three options are selected.

    d. Click OK to close the dialog box.

3 Explore Word Help.

    a. Click Help and view the Help commands.

    b. Click Search for Help on.

    c. Scroll through several topics and review them.

    d. In the search text box, type a topic about which you want more information.

    e. Click Show Topics to display related topics.

    f. Click a topic then click Go To. Read the information that appears in the How To window.

    g. Double-click the control menu box on the How To window to close it.

    h. Double-click the Help window control menu box to exit Help.

4 Close the document window and exit Word.

    a. Click File on the menu bar, then click Close.

    b. Click No if you see a message asking if you want to save your changes.

    c. Click File on the menu bar, then click Exit.

INDEPENDENT
CHALLENGE I

The Quick Preview command on the Help menu provides an on-line, animated tour of Word features, including many of the features you learned about in this unit. This tour also gives you an overview of the many different ways you can use Word to create documents of all types. To start the demonstration, click Help on the menu bar then click Quick Preview. Then select Getting Started and follow the instructions on the screen.

INDEPENDENT
CHALLENGE 2

You can use the keyboard or the mouse to move around in a document and to choose a command. Use on-line Help to learn about the keyboard shortcuts for opening a document and navigating in Word. Search for the Open command and display the topic for shortcut keys. Then use the shortcut keys to open the document you used earlier in this lesson, UNIT_1-1.DOC. Search for keyboard shortcuts and display the topic for using shortcut keys to move around in a Word document. After moving through the document, use a shortcut key to close the document *without saving it*.

Creating
AND EDITING A DOCUMENT

Now that you are familiar with the basics of the Word environment, you are ready to create a new document. After entering text in a new document, you can easily insert, delete, and replace text. You can also rearrange text by copying and moving selected text. ▶ At Nomad Ltd, Angela needs to create a letter to Nomad's shareholders. Her letter will include text that she will copy from another document, which was already prepared by a colleague in the Marketing Department. Before printing the document, Angela needs to check the document's spelling and preview the document to see how it will look when printed. ▶

Planning a document

Although Word makes it easy to modify documents after you have created them, it is always a good idea to plan the document before you begin typing it. Planning a document helps you work more effectively by helping you focus on the features you will need to use. Planning a document involves four areas: content, organization, tone, and format. Begin by determining what you want to say: in other words, identify the content of the document. Next, organize the ideas into a logical order in which they should be presented. With the content and organization clarified, you can begin writing using a tone that matches the content, purpose, and audience of the document. For example, the words you use in an announcement to a company picnic will be different in tone from a business letter requesting payment for an overdue invoice. Finally, you can make the document visually appealing, using formatting that emphasizes the ideas presented in the document and that is consistent with the content, tone, and organization. ▶ Angela wants to inform shareholders of an upcoming Annual Meeting and provide an overview of the year's highlights.

STEPS

1 **Choose the information and important points you want to cover in the document**
Angela writes down her ideas for the document, as shown in Figure 2-1.

2 **Decide how the information will be organized**
Because the information about the meeting is most important, Angela decides to present it first. The company highlights are included next. Later, if Angela decides to rearrange the structure of the document, she can use Word's editing features to move, copy, and cut text as needed.

3 **Choose the tone of the document**
Because the document is being sent to corporate shareholders, Angela will use a business-like tone. In addition, it has been a good year at Nomad Ltd, so Angela will also use a positive, enthusiastic tone intended to encourage shareholders to feel good about their investments in the company. Angela can edit the document as needed until she achieves exactly the tone she wants.

4 **Think about how you want the document to look**
To best communicate this information to her readers, Angela plans to use a straightforward business letter format for her document. The letter will include lists, directions, and a signature block. Each will require special formatting to distinguish these parts from the rest of the letter. If Angela changes her mind about the format of the document, she can make adjustments later.

FIGURE 2-1: Angela's document plan

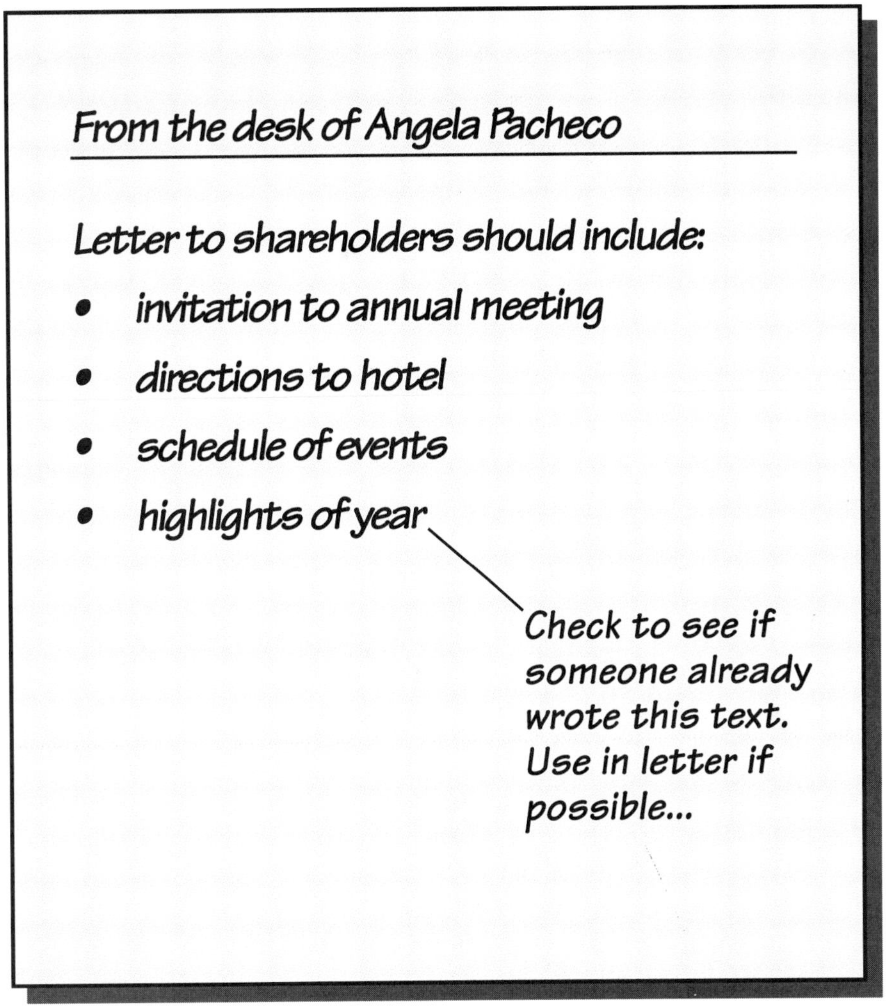

From the desk of Angela Pacheco

Letter to shareholders should include:

• invitation to annual meeting

• directions to hotel

• schedule of events

• highlights of year

Check to see if someone already wrote this text. Use in letter if possible...

Entering text and saving a document

When you start Word, the application opens a document window in which you can create a new document. You can begin by simply typing text at the insertion point. After entering text, you need to save the document so that it is stored permanently on disk. You save a document using the Save or Save As command on the File menu, or the Save button on the Standard toolbar. Table 2-1 shows the difference between the Save and Save As commands. ▶ Angela begins by typing the greeting and two paragraphs of her letter to Nomad Ltd's shareholders. After she types the text of her letter, she can save it.

1 **Start Word and insert your Student Disk in drive A**
   If you are unsure of how to start Word, refer to "Starting Word 6.0 for Windows" in Unit 1. Also, refer to the "Word 6.0 Screen Check" section on the "Read This Before You Begin Microsoft Word 6.0" page to make sure your Word screen is set up appropriately.

2 **At the insertion point, type Dear Shareholder:**
   The text appears to the left of the insertion point. The paragraph mark moves to the right as you type.

3 **Press [Enter] twice**
   Pressing [Enter] displays a paragraph mark at the end of the line, and moves the insertion point to the next line. The second paragraph mark creates a blank line.

4 **Type the two paragraphs of text shown in Figure 2-2; do not press [Enter] until you reach the end of a paragraph, then press [Enter] twice (at the end of the second paragraph, press [Enter] only once)**
   When you are typing and you reach the end of a line, Word automatically moves the text to the next line. This is called **word-wrap**. Pressing [Enter] twice inserts a blank line between paragraphs. Don't be concerned about making typing mistakes. Later in this unit, you will learn how to make revisions. Also, don't be concerned if your text wraps differently from the text shown in the figure. Exactly how text wraps can depend on the kind of monitor you are using or the type of printer you have selected. Next, Angela saves her letter.

5 **Click File on the menu bar then click Save As**
   The Save As dialog box opens. In this dialog box, you need to assign a name to the document you are creating, replacing the default filename supplied by Word.

6 **In the File Name text box, type SHRHOLDR**
   Your document name can contain up to eight characters. Word automatically adds the file extension .DOC to the filename. Also, note that it doesn't matter whether you enter the filename in uppercase or lowercase. Next, you need to instruct Word to save the file to your Student Disk.

7 **Click the Drives list arrow, then click a:**
   These lessons assume your Student Disk is in drive A. If you are using a different drive or storing your practice files on a network, click the appropriate drive. If you are not saving files to the MY_FILES directory of your Student Disk, or if you did not complete the exercises in "Microsoft Windows 3.1," you can skip Step 8.

8 **In the Directories list box, make sure the MY_FILES directory is selected**
   To select a directory, double-click the directory name. Compare the completed dialog box to Figure 2-3.

9 **Click OK**
   The document is saved with the name SHRHOLDR.

FIGURE 2-2:
Text in a Word
document

Blank line between
paragraphs

Text wraps automati-
cally to next line

Press [Enter] twice

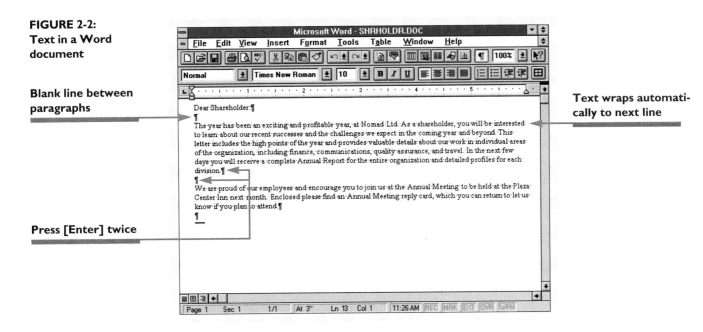

FIGURE 2-3:
Save As dialog box

Filename you provide

Directory for storing
files you save

Files on Student Disk

Drive containing
Student Disk

Click to display
other drives

Inserting spaces between sentences

When you first learned how to type, you might have been instructed to insert two spaces after a period between sentences. Because of advances in typography and the size and shape of text used in word processing applications, you need to type only one space between sentences.

TABLE 2-1: The difference between the Save and Save As commands

COMMAND	DESCRIPTION	PURPOSE
Save As	Saves file, requires input name	To save a file the first time, to change the filename, or to save the file for use in a different application. Useful for backups.
Save	Saves named file	To save any changes to the original file. Fast and easy—do this often to protect your work.

TROUBLE?

If you cannot see the nonprinting characters (spaces, tabs, and paragraph marks), click the Show/Hide ¶ button ▣ on the Standard toolbar. If not all of the nonprinting characters appear, choose Options from the Tools menu. Click the View tab, then in the Nonprinting Characters section, click All.■

QUICK **TIP**

The keyboard short-cut for saving a docu-ment is [Ctrl][S].■

Inserting and deleting text

After typing text, you'll often need to edit it by inserting new text or deleting text you want to remove. To insert text, place the insertion point where you want the new text to appear, then simply start typing. To delete text, place the insertion point next to the text you want to delete, then press [Backspace] to remove characters to the left of the insertion point, or press [Delete] to remove characters to the right of the insertion point. Whenever you insert or delete text, the existing text is automatically reformatted. ▶ First, Angela wants to add the inside address to her letter, then she'll make a few corrections to the letter using [Delete] and [Backspace] to remove individual characters of text.

1 Place the insertion point in front of the word "Dear" and type the following address, pressing **[Enter]** after each line:
Ms. Mary Ruiz [Enter]
321 Orange Way [Enter]
Green Valley, CA 90272 [Enter]

2 Press **[Enter]** again to insert a blank line above the greeting
Next, Angela wants to change the word "The" in the first sentence to "This."

3 Place the insertion point after the word "The" (but before the space) in the first sentence, press **[Backspace]**, then type **is**
The "e" to the left of the insertion point is removed, and the letters "is" are inserted. Next, Angela notices that the comma after the second occurrence of the word "year" is unnecessary, so she will delete this character as well.

4 Place the insertion point after the second occurrence of the word "year" (but before the comma) in the first sentence, then press **[Delete]**
The comma is removed. Next, Angela decides to add today's date to the beginning of the letter. She needs to move to the beginning of the document before she can insert it.

5 Press **[Ctrl][Home]** to place the insertion point at the beginning of the document
Notice that the status bar displays the position of the insertion point as you move around in the document. With the insertion point at the beginning of the document, Angela can quickly insert the date using the Date and Time command.

6 Click **Insert** on the menu bar, then click **Date and Time**
The Date and Time dialog box opens, as shown in Figure 2-4. In this dialog box, you can select the format in which the date and/or time will appear in your document. Word automatically displays the date based on your computer's system clock, so the dates you see in the dialog box might be different from those shown in the figure. For letters and other business correspondence, Angela prefers the fourth option in the list.

7 In the dialog box, click the **fourth option** in the list, then click **OK**
Today's date automatically appears in the document.

8 Press **[Enter]** twice
Compare your document to Figure 2-5; however, the date you see might be different.

9 Click **File** on the menu bar, then click **Save**
Your changes to the letter are saved in the document file. Because you already saved and named the document, the Save As dialog box does not open when you choose Save.

FIGURE 2-4: Date and Time dialog box

Select this date format

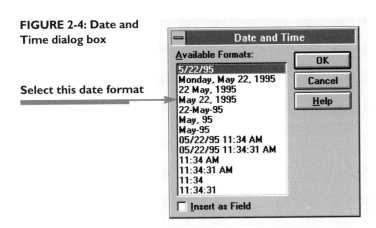

FIGURE 2-5: Letter after inserting and deleting text

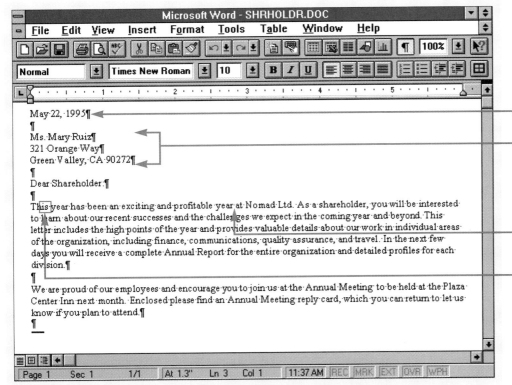

Inserted date

Inserted inside address

Comma deleted

Replaced text

Inserting date and time codes

When you use the Date and Time command, Word inserts a special code that displays the system date on your computer. Whenever you use the Print Preview or Print command, the date is automatically updated. When the insertion point is inside a code, the entire code appears shaded. This indicates that the text displayed is actually the result of a code.

TROUBLE?

If your typing overwrites existing text, check to see if the indicator "OVR" appears in the status bar. If it does, this means that Word is in Overtype mode. You need to switch back to Insert mode by pressing [Insert] or double-clicking OVR in the status bar, so that text you type does not overwrite existing text.

Selecting and replacing text

In addition to editing characters one at a time, you can also edit multiple characters, words, paragraphs, or the entire document. Most Word editing techniques require first selecting the text you want to edit. For example, to delete existing text and replace it with new text, you first select the text you want to remove then type the new text. This feature is called **Typing Replaces Selection**. Table 2-2 describes the different ways to select text. ▶ Next, Angela will use various techniques to select and replace text.

1 **Place the insertion point in front of the second occurrence of the word year in the first sentence and drag across the word**
The word is highlighted, indicating it is selected. Angela wants to replace the selection with the word "one" so that the word "year" is not used twice in the same sentence.

2 **Type one**
The word "one" replaces the selected word. Now Angela replaces several words with one word.

3 **Place the insertion point in front of the word please in the last sentence and drag across it and the next word, find, then release the mouse button**
Both words and the spaces are selected. The next operation you perform will affect the selected text. If you drag across too many words, drag back over the text to deselect it.

4 **Type is**
The word "is" replaces the selected text. Word automatically inserts the correct spacing and reformats the text after the insertion point. Angela decides that the word "summarizes" would be more accurate than the word "includes" in the third sentence.

5 **Double-click the word includes in the third sentence, then type summarizes**
The word "summarizes" replaces the selected text, along with the correct spacing. If you change your mind after making an editing change, you can reverse it with the Undo button on the Standard toolbar. Angela decides to use the Undo button to reinsert the word "includes."

6 **Click the Undo button ⟲ on the Standard toolbar**
Your editing action is reversed, and the word "includes" replaces the word "summarizes." Clicking the Undo button reverses the most recent action. The arrow next to the Undo button displays a list of all changes you've made since opening the document, so you can undo one or more changes. The Redo button reverses an action you've undone.

7 **Click the Redo button ⟳ on the Standard toolbar**
The word "summarizes" reappears. As with the Undo feature, the arrow next to the Redo button displays a list of changes you can redo.

8 **Position the pointer to the far left of the first line of the body of the letter until the pointer changes to ⟰ then click**
The first line of text is selected when you click next to the line in the selection bar. The **selection bar** is the area to the left of the text in your document, as shown in Figure 2-6.

9 **Click anywhere in the document to deselect the text, then click the Save button 🖫 on the Standard toolbar**
The first line is no longer selected. Whenever you want to deselect text, simply click in the document window. Clicking the Save button is the same as choosing Save from the File menu.

FIGURE 2-6:
Selected text and
selection bar

Selection bar

Selected text

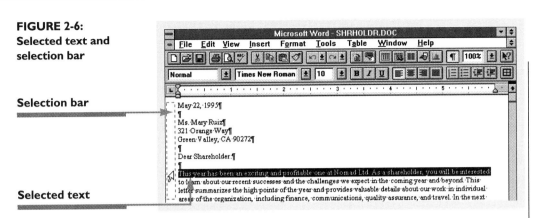

TROUBLE?

If text you type does not replace selected text, click Tools, click Options, click the Edit tab, then click to select the Typing Replaces Selection check box. Click OK to return to the document.■

TABLE 2-2: Mouse and keyboard selection techniques

SELECTING TEXT WITH THE MOUSE	DO THIS
A word	Double-click the word
A sentence	Press and hold [Ctrl] and click in the sentence
A paragraph	Triple-click in the paragraph, or double-click in the selection bar next to the paragraph
A line of text	Click in the selection bar next to the line
An entire document	Press and hold [Ctrl] and click anywhere in the selection bar, or triple-click in the selection bar
A vertical block of text	Press and hold [Alt] and drag through the text
A large amount of text	Place the insertion point at the beginning of the text, move to the end of the desired selection, then press and hold [Shift] and click

SELECTING TEXT WITH THE KEYBOARD	AT THE START OF THE SELECTION, PRESS	AT THE END OF THE SELECTION, PRESS
A character	[Shift][→]	[Shift][←]
A word	[Ctrl][Shift][→]	[Ctrl][Shift][←]
A paragraph	[Ctrl][Shift][↓]	[Ctrl][Shift][↑]
To the end/start of a line	[Shift][End]	[Shift][Home]
To the end/start of a document	[Ctrl][Shift][End]	[Ctrl][Shift][Home]
An entire document	[Ctrl][A]	
A vertical block of text	[Ctrl][Shift][F8] and select with the arrow keys	

Opening a document and saving it with a new name

In Unit 1, you opened an existing document, then closed it without saving changes. When you open a document and you want to work with it, but you want to make sure that no changes are made to it, you can save the document with a new name. This creates a copy of the document, leaving the original intact. ▶ Earlier Angela reviewed a document created by a colleague at Nomad Ltd. This document contains additional text Angela wants to use in her letter. So that she does not alter the original file for this other document, Angela opens the document and saves it with a new name. Then she can use the text in her saved copy of the document to add to her letter.

1 Click the **Open button** 📄 on the Standard toolbar
Word displays the Open dialog box, as shown in Figure 2-7. The MY_FILES directory is the current directory because this was the last directory you accessed (when you saved a file earlier in this unit). If you are not saving files to the MY_FILES directory, skip Step 2. Drive A should be the current directory.

2 Double-click the **a:** directory in the Directories list box to display the list of practice files stored on your Student Disk
When you double-click a new directory to make it the current directory, the files in the directory appear in the File Name list box.

3 Click the document named **UNIT_2-1.DOC** in the File Name list box, then click **OK**
The document UNIT_2-1.DOC appears in the document window, as shown in Figure 2-8. To keep this original file intact, Angela will save it with a new name, SUMMARY. Then she'll continue working with this copy of the original file.

4 Click **File** on the menu bar, then click **Save As**
The Save As dialog box opens, in which you can enter a new name for the document.

5 Make sure the Drives list box displays the drive containing your Student Disk
If you are not saving files to the MY_FILES directory, skip Step 6 and continue with Step 7.

6 Double-click the **MY_FILES** directory to make it the current directory

7 In the File Name text box, type **SUMMARY** then click **OK**
The document is saved with the new name, and the original document is closed.

FIGURE 2-7: Open dialog box

Files in current directory

Current directory

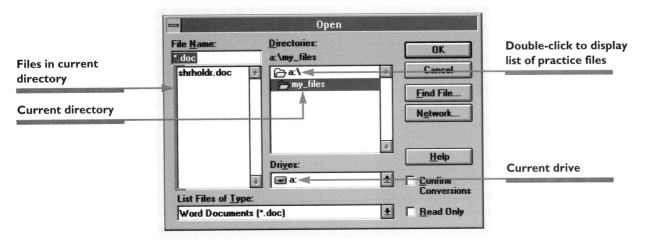

Double-click to display list of practice files

Current drive

FIGURE 2-8: Open Word document

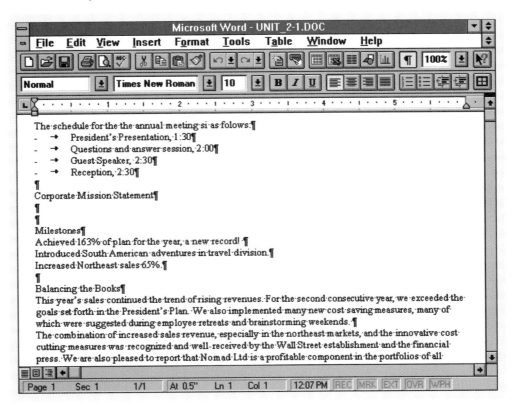

QUICK

You can double-click a filename in the Open dialog box to open the document. This is faster than clicking the filename then clicking OK.■

Copying and moving text

Moving and Copying Data

You can copy existing text that you want to reuse in a document, and you can remove text from its current location and place it elsewhere in a document. There are two ways to copy and move text: you can drag the text to a new location using the mouse, or you can use the Clipboard. The **Clipboard** is a temporary storage area for text and is available in any Windows application. Table 2-3 summarizes the techniques you can use to move and copy text using the Clipboard. ▶ Now that Angela has opened and reviewed the document created by her colleague, she can copy text from it to her letter. Angela displays both documents at once, in separate windows, so that she can work in both documents at the same time.

1 Click **Window** on the menu bar, then click **Arrange All**
Both documents appear in the application window, as shown in Figure 2-9. Each appears in its own document window, with its own scroll bars, rulers, and Minimize and Maximize buttons (these buttons only appear in the currently active document window). Angela wants to copy all the text from her colleague's document to her letter.

2 With the pointer in the selection bar of the SUMMARY document, triple-click the **left mouse button**
Triple-clicking in the selection bar selects the entire document.

3 Click the **Copy button** 🖳 on the Standard toolbar
The selected text is copied to the Clipboard. By placing text on the Clipboard (with either the Cut or Copy command), you can insert the text anywhere in the document as many times as you want. Angela wants to place this text before the last sentence in her letter.

4 Click in the SHRHOLDR document window to make it active, then place the insertion point in front of the last sentence, as shown in Figure 2-10

5 Click the **Paste button** 🖳 on the Standard toolbar
The copied text is inserted, but remains on the Clipboard until you copy or cut new text. Angela now wants to copy and move selected text in her letter. To make it easier to work in her document, Angela maximizes the SHRHOLDR document window.

6 Click anywhere in the SHRHOLDR document window, then click the **Maximize button**
With this document window maximized, Angela can see more of the document at once.

FIGURE 2-9:
Two open documents in the Word application window

Select all the text in this document

Highlighted title bar indicates active window

FIGURE 2-10:
Copying text from the Clipboard

Position insertion point here

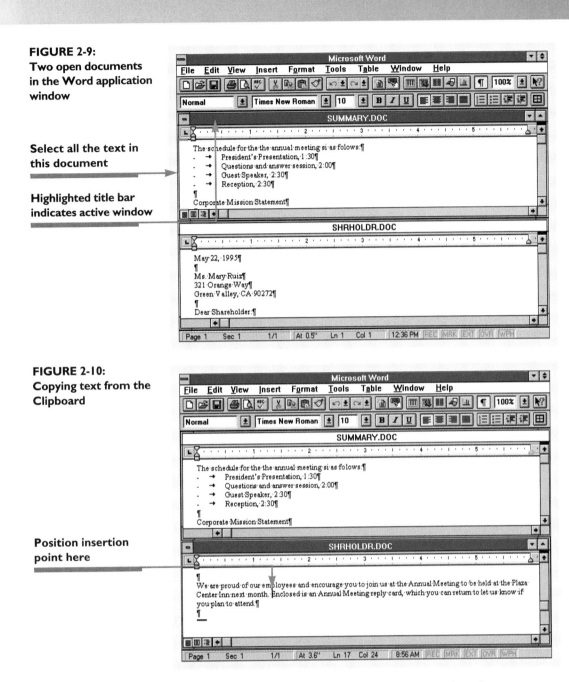

TABLE 2-3: Menu commands, buttons, and keyboard shortcuts for copying and moving text

ACTION	MENU COMMAND	WITH A BUTTON	WITH THE KEYBOARD
Cut selected text	Click Edit then click Cut to place the text on the Clipboard and remove the selection from the document		[Ctrl][X]
Copy selected text	Click Edit then click Copy to place the text on the Clipboard and retain the selection in the document		[Ctrl][C]
Paste	Click Edit then click Paste to paste the contents of the Clipboard at the insertion point		[Ctrl][V]

Copying and moving text, continued

First, Angela wants to copy the company name, Nomad Ltd, to other locations in the document.

7 Select the text **Nomad Ltd** in the first paragraph, then click the **Copy button** 📋 on the Standard toolbar

The selected text is copied to the Clipboard. Angela wants to place this text in front of the word "shareholder" in the next sentence.

8 Place the insertion point after the space in front of the word **shareholder**, then click the **Paste button** 📋 on the Standard toolbar

The text "Nomad Ltd" is inserted, as shown in Figure 2-11. Angela wants to insert the company name again, this time after the word "our" in the next paragraph.

9 Place the insertion point after the space after the word **our** in the next paragraph, then click 📋 on the Standard toolbar

The text Nomad Ltd is inserted. Angela now wants to move the last sentence to follow the schedule of events.

10 Press **[Ctrl][End]** to move quickly to the end of the document, then select the last sentence in the document

With the sentence selected, Angela uses the dragging method to move the text to the new location in the document.

11 Position the pointer over the selection, press and hold the mouse button until the pointer changes from I to ▷; *do not release the mouse button yet*

When you select only part of a document and hold down the mouse button, the text remains highlighted as you drag the mouse to move the text. If you want to copy selected text rather than move it, press and hold [Ctrl] first.

12 Drag the mouse up, scrolling through the document until you see the schedule of events, place the vertical bar of the pointer in the first line below the last event, then release the mouse button

The sentence is inserted. Compare your document to Figure 2-12. Angela decides this is a good time to save her work.

13 In the letter document, click the **Save button** 💾 on the Standard toolbar

The changes you made to the SHRHOLDR letter are saved.

FIGURE 2-11:
Document with
inserted text

Inserted text

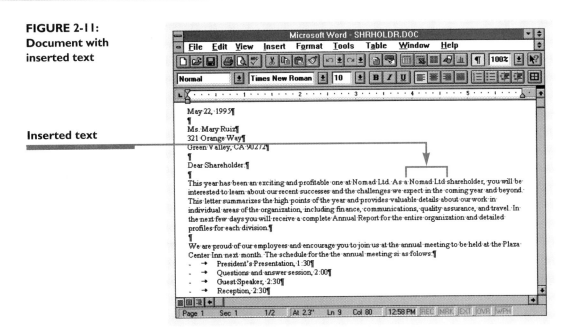

FIGURE 2-12:
Completed document

Copied text

Moved text

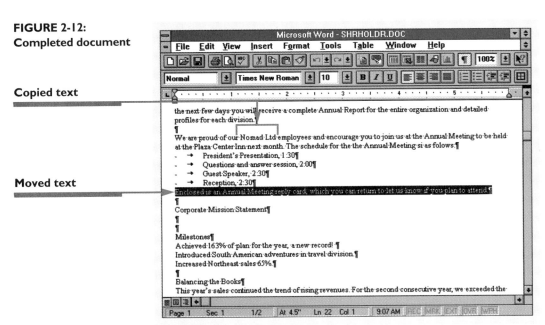

The Delete key vs. the Cut command

Pressing [Delete] is not the same as using the Cut command. The Cut command places the selected text on the Clipboard after removing it from the document. Pressing [Delete] only removes the text; the text is not on the Clipboard and is not available for pasting.

TROUBLE?

If the selected text does not move when you try to drag, click Tools, click Options, click the Edit tab, then click to select the Drag-and-Drop Text Editing check box.■

Correcting spelling errors

Word's Spelling command identifies and corrects spelling errors and repeated words (such as "the the"). This command identifies as misspelled any words not found in the Word dictionary, including proper nouns. From a list of suggested spellings, you can choose the spelling you want to use. ▶ Before Angela prints her letter, she checks that it contains no spelling errors.

1   Press **[Ctrl][Home]** to place the insertion point at the beginning of the document, then click the **Spelling button** 🔤 on the Standard toolbar
The Spelling dialog box opens, showing the first error located in the document—the word "Ruiz," as shown in Figure 2-13. Figure 2-13 also describes the options in the Spelling dialog box. The identified word is a proper noun and is not misspelled so Angela ignores this error.

2   Click **Ignore** in the Spelling dialog box
Word identifies "Ltd" as the next misspelled word. Suggested spellings are displayed in the Suggestions list box. Because this is part of the company name and appears often in company correspondence, Angela decides to add this word to the Word dictionary.

3   Click **Add** to add the word "Ltd" to the dictionary
The next time the Spelling command encounters this word, it will not be identified as misspelled. Next, the Spelling dialog box indicates that the word "the" is repeated. The options available in the dialog box change when Word identifies a repeated word. Angela deletes the repeated word.

4   Click **Delete** to delete the second occurrence of the word
The Spelling command identifies "si" as the next misspelled word. Because this is a typing mistake Angela makes frequently, she creates an **AutoCorrect entry** for this word so that this misspelling will be corrected automatically as she types it.

5   Click **AutoCorrect** to create an AutoCorrect entry
If someone has already created an AutoCorrect entry for "si," you will see a message asking if you want to replace the existing entry. Click OK to continue.

    The next time Angela types "si" followed by a space, Word will supply the corrected word "is." See the related topic "More about AutoCorrect" for additional information. The word "folows" is identified as misspelled and a suggested correction appears in the Change To text box.

6   Click **Change** in the Spelling dialog box to replace "folows"
A message box opens, indicating that the spell check process is now complete.

7   Click **OK** to close the dialog box and return to the document
Angela decides to add one more paragraph of text and to test her AutoCorrect entry.

8   Place the insertion point in front of the paragraph mark below "Corporate Mission Statement," then type the following text (make sure you type the incorrect word "si" and watch how AutoCorrect corrects it:
Nomad Ltd si a national sporting-goods retailer dedicated to delivering high-quality adventure sporting gear and clothing.

9   Click the **Save button** 💾 on the Standard toolbar

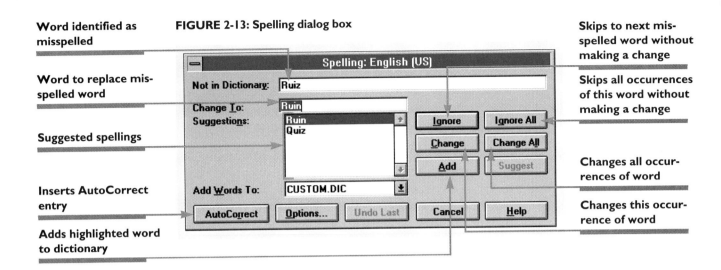

Word identified as misspelled

FIGURE 2-13: Spelling dialog box

Skips to next misspelled word without making a change

Word to replace misspelled word

Skips all occurrences of this word without making a change

Suggested spellings

Inserts AutoCorrect entry

Changes all occurrences of word

Adds highlighted word to dictionary

Changes this occurrence of word

More about AutoCorrect

Word provides several AutoCorrect entries for correcting some common typing errors. It also provides the correct capitalization if you type two capital letters at the beginning of a word, and corrects the capitalization when you type the names of days. With the AutoCorrect feature, you can specify the kind of quotation marks to use in the document, and that the first character in a sentence should be capitalized. You can add AutoCorrect entries when Word locates a misspelled word in the Spelling dialog box, or you can click Tools then click AutoCorrect to display the AutoCorrect dialog box, as shown in Figure 2-14. In this dialog box, you can select or deselect the AutoCorrect features, and add entries at any time.

FIGURE 2-14:
AutoCorrect dialog box

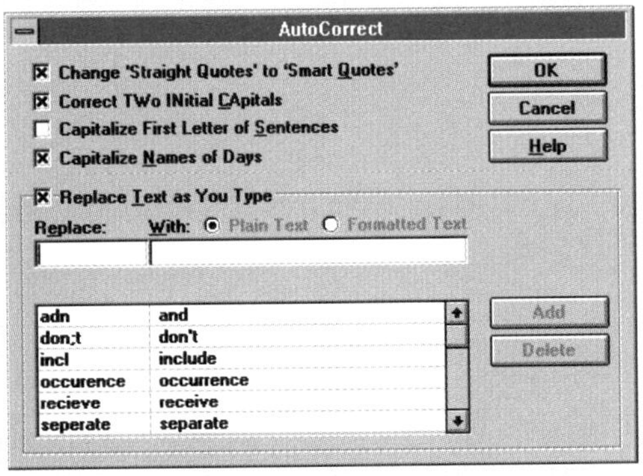

TROUBLE?

If the Spelling command does not identify the same misspelled words as described in this lesson, it means that someone else has already added words to the dictionary on this computer or that you made additional typing mistakes when you typed the letter. Correct any other errors identified in the spell check, as appropriate.∎

Previewing a document

After proofreading and correcting your document, you are almost ready to print it. Before you do, it is a good idea to display the document using the Print Preview command. In print preview, you can easily check your page margins and the overall appearance of your document. If you notice additional changes you would like to make, you can get a close-up view of the page and make final changes before printing. ▶ Angela is now ready to preview her letter to see how it will look before printing it.

1 **Click the Print Preview button** 🔍 **on the Standard toolbar**
The document appears in the Preview window, as shown in Figure 2-15. The size of the page you see depends on the number and size of pages displayed the last time someone used the Print Preview command. If you see more than one page, click the One Page button 🔲 on the Print Preview toolbar. As she views the document, Angela realizes she needs to get a close-up view of the schedule of events to examine it more closely.

2 **Click the page near the schedule of events**
Notice that the pointer changes to 🔍 when you position it in the document. The document is magnified, as shown in Figure 2-16. In print preview you can make quick changes without returning to the document window first. Angela decides to add extra space between the schedule of events and the next line of text.

3 **Click the Magnifier button** 🔍 **on the Print Preview toolbar**
The Magnifier pointer changes to the insertion point when it is in text. Now you can edit the text.

4 **Place the insertion point in front of the word Enclosed after the schedule, then press [Enter]**
A blank line is inserted. Next, Angela decides to break the document into two parts. The part on the first page is the letter, and the part on the second page is the summary of the year's highlights. She decides to insert a page break between the two parts of the document.

5 **Place the insertion point in front of the word Corporate, click Insert on the menu bar, then click Break**
The Break dialog box opens. See the related topic "About page breaks" for more information.

6 **Make sure the Page Break button is selected, then click OK**
All the text after the insertion point now appears on the second page. Angela wants to view both pages of the document in print preview.

7 **Click the Multiple Pages button** ▦ **on the Print Preview toolbar, then drag to select two pages**
You see both pages of the document.

8 **Click the Close button on the Print Preview toolbar**
The Preview window closes and you return to the document in the normal view.

9 **Click the Save button** 💾 **on the Standard toolbar**

FIGURE 2-15: Document in print preview

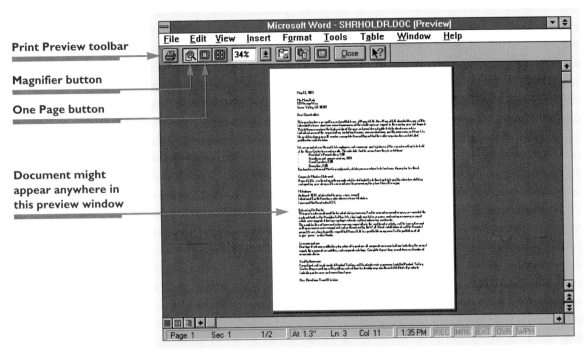

Print Preview toolbar

Magnifier button

One Page button

Document might appear anywhere in this preview window

FIGURE 2-16: Close-up view of document

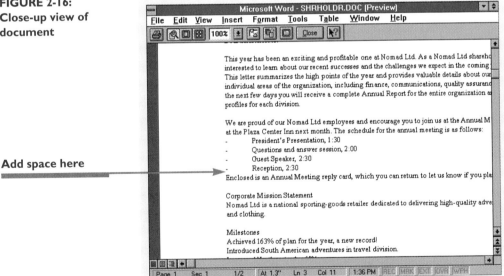

Add space here

About page breaks

When the amount of text requires more than one page, Word automatically inserts a **soft page break** and formats the text onto a new page. A light dotted line appears between pages to represent a soft page break in your document. If you want to specify where a page break should occur, you can insert a **hard**, or **manual, page break**. A hard page break is represented by a darker dotted line between pages with the words "Page Break" in the center of the dotted line. You cannot delete a soft page break, but you can delete a hard page break by selecting the dotted line and pressing [Delete].

QUICK **TIP**

A quick way to display the document in print preview is to press [Ctrl][F2].■

Printing a document

Printing a document is as simple as clicking the Print button on the Standard toolbar (or the Print Preview toolbar). However, to take advantage of many printing options, use the Print command on the File menu. This command displays the Print dialog box in which you can select the print options you want to use, depending on your needs and the size of the document you want to print. See Table 2-4 to learn more about printing options.▶ Now that Angela has proofread and corrected her document, she will add a closing and then print the document.

1 Place the insertion point in the paragraph mark at the end of the first page, above the page break line, press **[Enter]**, then type the following text (be sure to press [Enter] after each line)
Sincerely, [Enter]
[Enter]
Angela Pacheco [Enter]
Marketing Division Manager [Enter]
Nomad Ltd [Enter]

2 Click the **Save button** 🖫 on the Standard toolbar
The changes are saved in the document. Now Angela is ready to print, so she makes sure the printer is on and contains paper.

3 Click **File** on the menu bar, then click **Print**
The Print dialog box opens, as shown in Figure 2-17. In this dialog box, you can specify the print options you want to use when you print your document. The name of the printer and the options you have available might be different, depending on the kind of printer you have set up on your computer.

4 In the Copies text box, type **2**
The entry "2" replaces the default entry of "1." You will print a copy of this document for yourself and for your instructor.

5 Click **OK**
The Print dialog box closes, and your document is printed.

6 Click **File** on the menu bar, then click **Close**
The SHRHOLDR document closes. The SUMMARY document appears in the document window. This document was open while you worked on the letter. You can close this document as well.

7 Click **File** on the menu bar, then click **Close**
A dialog box might open asking if you want to save changes to the SUMMARY document.

8 Click **Yes** to save changes to the document

9 Click **File** on the menu bar, then click **Exit** to close the Word application

FIGURE 2-17: Print dialog box

Specifies what you want to print

Number of copies to print

Pages that you want to print

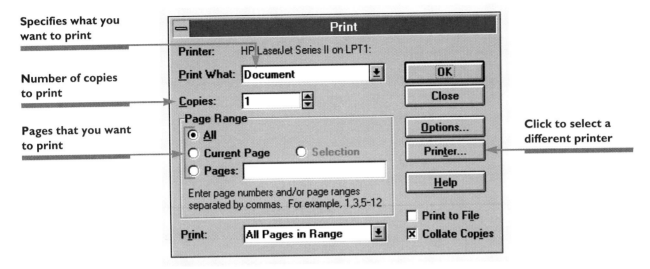

Click to select a different printer

TABLE 2-4: Printing options

PRINT OPTIONS	DESCRIPTION
Printer	Displays the name of the selected printer and print connection
Print What	Prints the document (default), or only the summary information, annotations, styles, or other text associated with the document
Copies	Specifies the number of copies to print
Page Range	Specifies the pages to print: • *All*: prints the complete document • *Current Page*: prints the page with the insertion point or the selected page • *Selection*: prints selected text only • *Pages*: prints user-specified pages (separate single pages with a comma, a range of pages with a hyphen)
Print	Specifies the print order for the page range: All Pages in Range, Odd Pages, Even Pages
Print to File	Print a document to a new file instead of a printer
Collate Copies	Prints all pages of the first copy before printing subsequent copies, when multiple copies are selected (not available on all printers)

QUICK **TIP**

The shortcut key for the Print command is [Ctrl][P].■

TROUBLE?

If you are not connected to a printer, ask your technical support person or instructor for assistance.■

CONCEPTSREVIEW

Describe each of the parts of the Spelling dialog box in Figure 2-18.

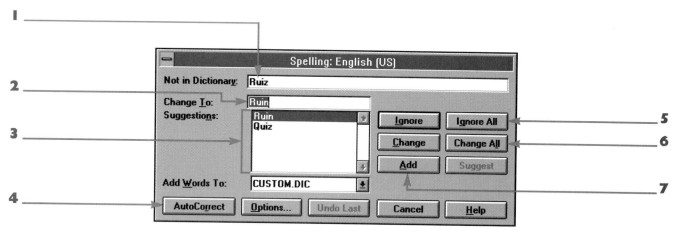

FIGURE 2-18

Match each of the following terms with the statement that best describes its function.

8 Selecting text and typing text in its place

9 Typing text between existing text

10 Removing text to the right or left of the insertion point

11 Temporary holding area for text to be pasted

12 Duplicating text in multiple locations

13 Removing text to be inserted in another location

14 Inserting the contents of the Clipboard

    a. Deleting

    b. Clipboard

    c. Replacing

    d. Copying

    e. Inserting

    f. Pasting

    g. Cutting

Select the best answer from the list of choices.

15 Which of the following methods is NOT a way to select text?

    a. Clicking in the selection bar

    b. Dragging across text

    c. Double-clicking a word with the left mouse button

    d. Dragging text to the selection bar

16 Which of the following statements about the selection bar is NOT true?

    a. You can select the entire document from the selection bar.

    b. You can select part of a line from the selection bar.

    c. You can select a line from the selection bar.

    d. You must always use the mouse to select text from the selection bar.

17 Which key do you press to remove text to the left of the insertion point?

    a. [Backspace]

    b. [Delete]

    c. [Cut]

    d. [Overtype]

18 To place text on the Clipboard, you must first

    a. Click the Copy button

    b. Click the Cut button

    c. Click the Paste button

    d. Select the text

19 How many times can you use the Paste button to insert the contents of the Clipboard?

a. Twice

b. Once

c. Depends on the memory of the computer

d. Unlimited number of times

20 How many previous actions can you undo?

a. Two

b. One

c. All actions since the last time you saved the document

d. All actions since you opened the document

21 To display two open documents at once, you use which menu and command?

a. Click Window on the menu bar, then click Arrange All

b. Click Window on the menu bar, then click Split

c. Click Window on the menu bar, then click New Window

d. Click File on the menu bar, click Print Preview, then click Multiple Pages

22 What keys do you press to move the insertion point to the first character in a document?

a. [Ctrl][Home]

b. [Home]

c. [Alt][Page Up]

d. [Shift][Tab]

23 For most efficient document creation, when is the best time to proofread your document?

a. Just before printing

b. As soon as you have finished typing it

c. Before rearranging text

d. As you type, so you don't make any mistakes

24 What option is NOT available in the Spelling dialog box when a spelling error is identified?

a. Add the word to the dictionary

b. Add an AutoCorrect entry

c. Delete the incorrect word

d. Choose a suggested spelling

25 When does AutoCorrect correct your typing mistake?

a. When you press [Spacebar] after typing the word incorrectly

b. When you type a misspelled word

c. When you click the AutoCorrect button in the Spelling dialog box

d. When you click the AutoCorrect button on the Formatting toolbar

26 Which statement best describes the AutoCorrect feature?

a. Word comes with hundreds of AutoCorrect entries.

b. There must be an AutoCorrect entry for each typing mistake you want corrected automatically.

c. AutoCorrect "knows" what you want to type and types it for you.

d. AutoCorrect corrects grammatical errors as you make them.

27 In print preview, how do you get a close-up view of a page?

a. Click the Print Preview button

b. Click the Close button

c. Click the page with the Magnifier pointer

d. Click the One Page button

APPLICATIONSREVIEW

1 Create a new document and save it.

a. Start Word and complete the Word screen check procedure described on the "Read This Before You Begin Microsoft Word 6.0" page. Make sure you insert your Student Disk in the disk drive.

b. At the insertion point, type a short letter to a local business describing your interest in learning more about the company and requesting a copy of their annual report. Don't type the inside address or a closing yet. For a greeting, type "To Whom It May Concern:".

c. For a closing type "Sincerly," then press [Enter] twice. Be sure to misspell the word so that you can correct it later.

d. Click File on the menu bar, then click Save As.

e. Make the MY_FILES directory active on your Student Disk.

f. In the File Name text box, type NEWLTTR then click OK.

2 Insert and delete text.

a. Place the insertion point at the beginning of the document. Now type the inside address. Use whatever contact name, title, company name, and address that you want.

b. Press [Enter] twice, then type your name and press [Enter]. Then type your street address and press [Enter]. Type your city, state and zip code and press [Enter] again. Then type your phone number.

c. Use [Backspace] to delete your phone number. Press [Enter] once more.

3 Select and replace text.

   a. Select the text "To Whom It May Concern," then type "Dear" followed by the name of the recipient of the letter; for example, Mr. Martin.

   b. Select the last word of the document, then press [Delete] to delete the entire word.

   c. Click the Undo button to restore the original text.

   d. Use selecting and replacing techniques to correct any mistakes in your letter.

4 Copy and move text.

   a. Use the two different copying techniques (using the Clipboard, and using the mouse and [Ctrl] to drag text) to copy the first sentence to the end of the document. Use the Undo button to reverse each action.

   b. Use the two different moving techniques (using the Clipboard, and using the mouse to drag text) to move the first sentence to the end of the document. Use the Undo button to reverse each action.

   c. Select your name and address at the beginning of the document (include the paragraph mark before your name) and move this text to the end of the document using either the mouse method or the Clipboard method.

   d. Click the Save button on the Standard toolbar to save your document.

5 Correct spelling in a document.

   a. Click the Spelling button on the Standard toolbar and correct any spelling errors.

   b. Add your name to the custom dictionary, if Word identifies it as misspelled.

   c. Add "Sincerly" as an AutoCorrect entry so that Word will provide the correct spelling "Sincerely" automatically. (If this AutoCorrect entry already exists, add an AutoCorrect entry of your choice after completing the spell check, using the AutoCorrect dialog box.)

   d. Click OK to close the Spelling dialog box and return to the document.

   e. Save your changes.

6 Preview a document.

   a. Click the Print Preview button on the Standard toolbar.

   b. Click the page near the signature.

   c. Click the Magnifier button on the Print Preview toolbar.

   d. Select the text under your name then type "Public Relations."

   e. Click the One Page button on the Print Preview toolbar.

   f. Click the Close button on the Print Preview toolbar.

   g. Save your changes.

7 Print a document.

   a. Click File on the menu bar, then click Print.

   b. In the Copies box, type 2.

   c. Click OK.

   d. Click File on the menu bar, then click Close.

   e. Click File on the menu bar, then click Exit.

INDEPENDENT
CHALLENGE 1

Suppose you are the fundraising coordinator for a local theater company, called Lightwell Players. In response to a request for information from a potential corporate sponsor, create a new document that is a short letter describing the benefits of being a sponsor. To end your letter, open one of the documents you used in this unit. Then copy the last paragraph and the closing with your signature to the end of your letter. Edit this copied text to include your name, the appropriate title (fundraising coordinator), and company name (Lightwell Players). Save the document with the name LGHTWELL.DOC to the MY_FILES directory on your Student Disk. Preview and print the document, then close it.

INDEPENDENT
CHALLENGE 2

As an account representative for At Your Service Temps, a temporary office services company, you drafted a letter describing the corporate discount program to a current customer. Open the document named UNIT_2-2.DOC from your Student Disk, then save it as TEMPS.DOC to your MY_FILES directory. Check the spelling in the document. Add the name of the newsletter to the dictionary. Create AutoCorrect entries for typographical errors, such as "haev." Save your changes to the document. Preview the document, then print it. Close the document and exit Word.

UNIT 3

OBJECTIVES

▶ Format text

▶ Align text with tabs

▶ Format paragraphs

▶ Create bulleted and numbered lists

▶ Format a document with AutoFormat and the Style Gallery

▶ Modify styles

▶ Apply borders and shading

▶ Format a paragraph with a drop cap

▶ Adjust document margins

Formatting
A DOCUMENT

So far you've used Word to enter, edit, and rearrange text in a document. In this unit, you'll use Word's formatting capabilities to change the appearance of text on the page. Because Word is a **WYSIWYG** application (pronounced wizzy-wig, it stands for **W**hat **Y**ou **S**ee **I**s **W**hat **Y**ou **G**et), your document will print with the same formatting that you see displayed in the document window. ▶ Angela needs to format her letter to Nomad Ltd's shareholders to emphasize important topics. She's also been asked to improve the appearance of the summary of highlights, which is now a separate document. ▶

Formatting text

Formatting text means changing the appearance of the letters and words in your document. The text format settings you can change are summarized in Table 3-1. Basic formatting options (such as bold, italics, font, and font size) are available on the Formatting toolbar, shown in Figure 3-1. Additional formatting options are available with the Font command on the Format menu, which displays the Font dialog box shown in Figure 3-2. ▶Angela begins formatting her letter to Nomad's shareholders by emphasizing selected text.

1 Start Word and insert your Student Disk in drive A

See the instructions in Unit 1 if you are unsure of how to start Word. Also, refer to the "Word 6.0 Screen Check" section on the "Read This Before You Begin Microsoft Word 6.0" page to make sure your Word screen is set up appropriately.

2 Open the document named UNIT_3-1.DOC from your Student Disk and save it as COVER.DOC to your MY_FILES directory

This document contains Angela's letter. Angela made additional revisions to the letter by adding two lists and removing the schedule because it has not been finalized yet. To draw attention to the location of the Annual Meeting, Angela decides to format this text in italics.

3 Select the first occurrence of the text **Plaza Center Inn** in the third paragraph, then click the **Italic button** 𝐼 on the Formatting toolbar

The text now appears in italics. Next, Angela decides to bold the company name.

4 Select the first occurrence of the text **Nomad Ltd** in the first paragraph, then click the **Bold button** **B** on the Formatting toolbar

Deselect the text to see that it now appears in bold. Angela decides to emphasize this text even more by changing the font.

5 Select the text again, click the **Font list arrow** on the Formatting toolbar, then click **Arial**

The text appears in the Arial font. The fonts available in the Font list box depend on the fonts installed on your computer. Arial is one of the Windows TrueType fonts, designated by a double "T" in the Font list. **TrueType fonts** display text as it will appear when printed. Angela thinks that the characters in the company name are too large, so she decides to reduce the font size of this text.

6 With the same text still selected, click the **Font Size list arrow** on the Formatting toolbar, then click **9**

The selected text appears in 9 point type. Because Angela wants all occurrences of the company name to be formatted this way, she uses the Format Painter to copy the formatting to the other occurrences.

7 With the same words still selected, double-click the **Format Painter button** 🖌 on the Standard toolbar

Word's **Format Painter** copies the formatting of selected text to the next text you select. By double-clicking the button instead of simply clicking, this feature remains in effect so that you can select and change multiple occurrences of text. Notice that the pointer changes to 🖌𝐼.

8 Drag across each occurrence of Nomad Ltd in the document, except in the signature block at the end of the letter

The formatting of the selected text is copied to the text you drag across. Scroll to the top of the screen and compare your document to Figure 3-3.

9 Click 🖌 to deactivate the Format Painter feature, then click the **Save button** 💾 on the Standard toolbar to save your changes

FIGURE 3-1: Text formatting buttons on Formatting toolbar

Font

Font list arrow

Font size

Font Size list arrow

Underline

Italic

Bold

FIGURE 3-2:
Font dialog box

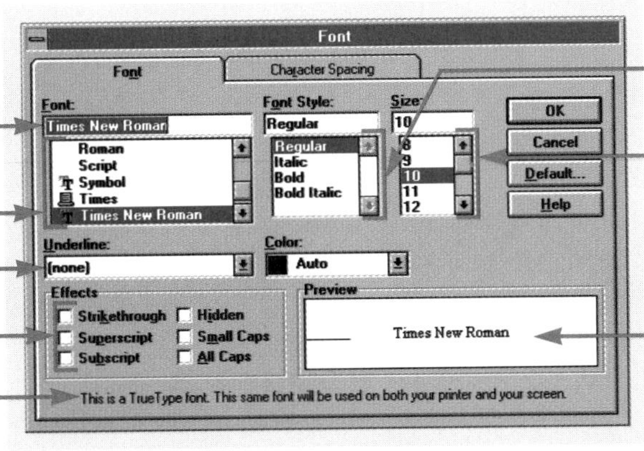

Currently selected font

Fonts available on
your computer

Underlining options

Effects options

Description of font

Font Style options

Font Size options

Example of
formatted text

FIGURE 3-3:
Formatted letter

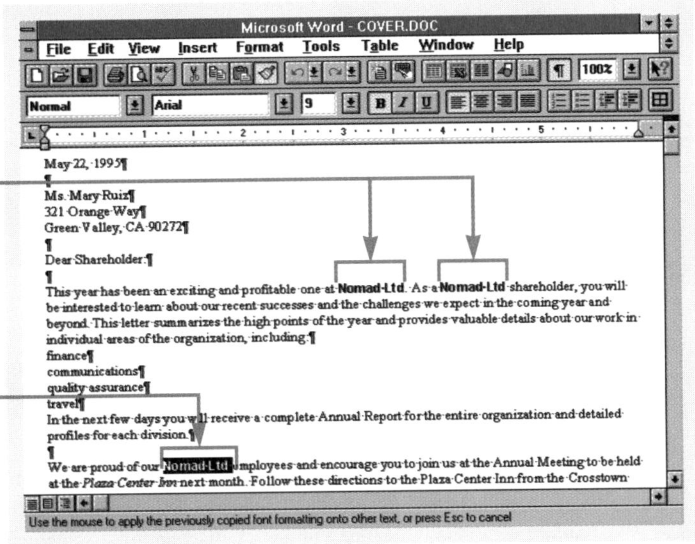

Bold, Arial, 9pt

TABLE 3-1: Text formatting options

SETTING	DESCRIPTION
Font	The name given to a collection of characters (letters, numerals, symbols, and punctuation marks) with a specific design. This text appears in a font named Arial. This text appears in a font named Times New Roman.
Font Size	The physical size of text, measured in points (pts). A point is $\frac{1}{72}$". The bigger the number of points, the larger the font size.
Font Style	The appearance of text as **bold**, *italicized*, or underlined, or any combination of these formats.
Effects	The appearance of text as SMALL CAPS, ALL CAPS, hidden text, strikethrough, subscript ($_{subscript}$), or superscript (^{superscript}).

Aligning text with tabs

Another way to change the appearance of text is to use tabs to align or indent text. When you press [Tab], the insertion point moves to the next tab stop. By default, tab stops are located at every half inch, but you can use the horizontal ruler (Figure 3-4) to position and create new tab stops. Table 3-2 describes the four different types of tabs and their corresponding tab markers as they appear on the ruler. ► Angela has received the final schedule of events for the Annual Meeting and would like to include it in the letter. To make the schedule easier to read, she uses tabs to align the events and the corresponding start times. First, she sets the tab stops on the ruler for the first line of the schedule.

1 **Make sure the tab alignment selector at the left end of the ruler displays the left-aligned tab marker (see Figure 3-4)**

If the left-aligned tab marker is not displayed, click the tab alignment selector until the left-aligned tab marker appears (see Table 3-2). The left-aligned tab is the default alignment for tab stops.

2 **Place the insertion point in front of the paragraph mark above the last sentence of the letter, then in the horizontal ruler click the ¾" mark**

A left-aligned tab marker appears where you clicked in the ruler. Next Angela wants to align the start times so the right edges are aligned evenly under each other. To do this, she selects the right-aligned tab marker from the tab alignment selector before placing another tab stop.

3 **Click the tab alignment selector until you see the right-aligned tab marker**

Each time you click the tab alignment selector, the tab marker changes to represent a new alignment for the next tab stop you place. With the right-aligned tab marker selected, Angela places a new tab stop on the ruler.

4 **In the horizontal ruler, click the 3" mark**

A right-aligned tab marker appears where you clicked in the ruler, as shown in Figure 3-5. This means that the right edge of text that appears after a tab character in this line will be aligned with this tab stop. With the tab stops set in the ruler, Angela is ready to enter the schedule of events.

5 **Press [Tab] then type Board of Directors meeting**

The left edge of the text is positioned under the tab stop at the ¾" mark. Next, type the time this event is scheduled.

6 **Press [Tab] then type 11:30**

The right edge of the time is positioned under the next tab stop.

7 **Press [Enter] and continue typing the remaining events and times shown in Figure 3-6**

The new line retains the tab settings you created in the previous line. Be sure to press [Tab] before each event and before each time and press [Enter] at the end of each line. Notice that a nonprinting character appears each time you pressed [Tab] or [Enter].

8 **Click the Save button 🖫 on the Standard toolbar**

Tab alignment selector showing default left-aligned tab marker

Default tab stop

Left-aligned tab marker in ruler

FIGURE 3-4: Horizontal ruler

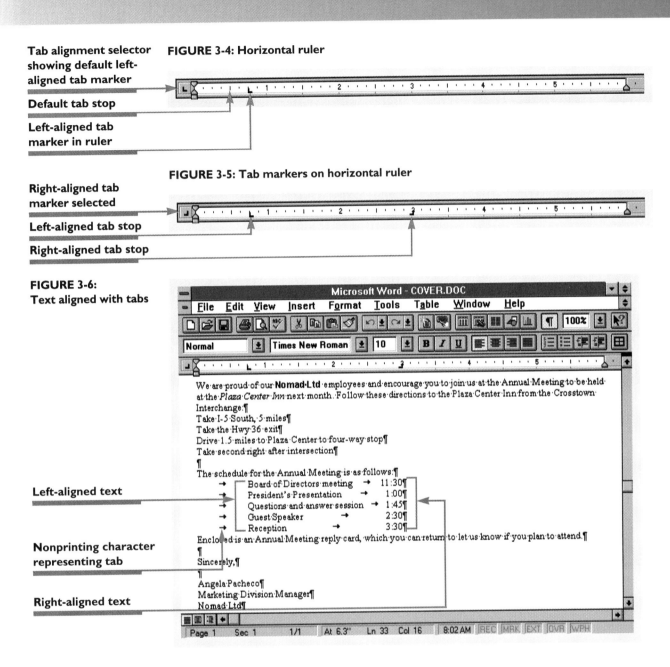

Right-aligned tab marker selected

Left-aligned tab stop

Right-aligned tab stop

FIGURE 3-5: Tab markers on horizontal ruler

FIGURE 3-6: Text aligned with tabs

Left-aligned text

Nonprinting character representing tab

Right-aligned text

TABLE 3-2: Different types of tabs

ALIGNMENT	DESCRIPTION	BUTTON
Left	Text aligns at the left and extends to the right of the tab stop	
Center	Text aligns at the middle of the tab stop, extending an equal distance to the left and right of the stop	
Right	Text aligns at the right and extends to the left of the tab stop	
Decimal	Text aligns at the decimal point; text before the decimal extends to the left, and text after extends to the right	

TROUBLE?

If you have difficulty getting the tab marker to appear, try clicking below the hash marks (small lines) or numbers on the ruler.■

Formatting paragraphs

In addition to formatting text, you can also format paragraphs. **Paragraph formatting** refers to the spacing, alignment, and indentation of text in paragraphs, as summarized in Table 3-3. Common paragraph formatting commands are available on the Formatting toolbar, as shown in Figure 3-7; however, additional formatting options are available when you choose the Paragraph command from the Format menu. ▶ Angela wants to improve the appearance of her letter by changing the formatting of certain paragraphs. First, she decides to align the date with the right margin.

I   Place the insertion point in the line that contains the date, then click the **Align Right button** 📄 on the Formatting toolbar

The date is aligned at the right margin of the page. You do not need to select the entire line or paragraph to apply paragraph formatting because paragraph formatting affects the entire current paragraph—that is, the one containing the insertion point. Angela realizes that the signature block at the end of the letter should be closer to the right margin, so that its right edge appears aligned under the right edge of the date.

2   Select the lines beginning with "Sincerely" and ending with the company name, then drag the left indent marker (the rectangle below the triangles on the left edge of the horizontal ruler) to the 4¼" mark, as shown in Figure 3-8

The text moves to align under the 4¼" mark. Next, Angela wants to make the schedule of events easier to read by increasing the spacing before and after each paragraph that makes up the schedule.

3   Select all the paragraphs for the schedule of events

Select these lines quickly by clicking in the selection bar to the left of the first line, then drag to select the remaining lines.

4   Click **Format** on the menu bar, then click **Paragraph**

The Paragraph dialog box opens, as shown in Figure 3-9. Make sure the Indents and Spacing tab is selected. The Preview box displays an example of text in the current settings. Because Spacing options provide more precise spacing between paragraphs than using extra paragraph marks, Angela will use the Spacing options to increase the spacing before and after each selected paragraph to 3 pts.

5   In the Spacing section, select the **0** in the Before text box, then type **3**

You can type a specific number of points in the Before and After text boxes, or you can click the arrows to increase or decrease spacing in increments of 6 pts.

6   Select the **0** in the After text box, type **3**, then click **OK**

The letter now shows the increased spacing before and after the paragraphs in the schedule of events. Compare your document to Figure 3-10.

7   Click the **Save button** 💾 on the Standard toolbar

TABLE 3-3:
Paragraph formatting options

SETTING	DESCRIPTION
Line Spacing	The amount of space between lines within a paragraph
Spacing Before and After	The amount of space before the first line and after the last line of a paragraph
Indentation	The beginning and/or end of lines of text in a paragraph in relation to the left and right margins
Alignment	The distribution of text within a paragraph between the left and right margins

FIGURE 3-7: Paragraph formatting buttons on the Formatting toolbar

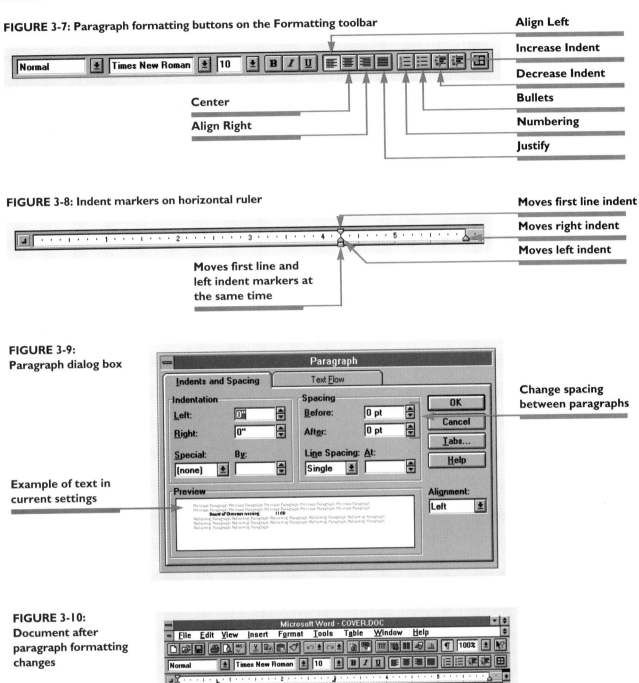

Align Left

Increase Indent

Decrease Indent

Bullets

Numbering

Justify

Center

Align Right

FIGURE 3-8: Indent markers on horizontal ruler

Moves first line indent

Moves right indent

Moves left indent

Moves first line and left indent markers at the same time

FIGURE 3-9:
Paragraph dialog box

Change spacing between paragraphs

Example of text in current settings

FIGURE 3-10:
Document after paragraph formatting changes

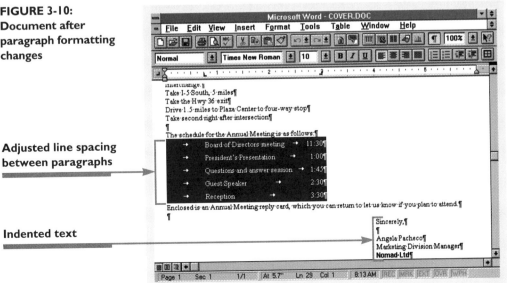

Adjusted line spacing between paragraphs

Indented text

Creating bulleted and numbered lists

With Word you can create bulleted and numbered lists easily and quickly. The Numbering button on the Formatting toolbar lets you number selected paragraphs, starting with 1. With the Bullets button, you can insert a bullet in front of each item in a list. A **bullet** is a small symbol, such as a solid circle or some other shape, that marks each item. Adding bullets or numbers to a list makes it easier to identify each item. Generally, you use numbered lists to show a sequence, and bulleted lists to identify nonsequential items in a list. ▶ Angela decides to draw attention to the list of departments by formatting it with bullets; then she'll add numbers to the directions to the Annual Meeting to clarify the sequence.

1. Select the list of department names starting with "finance," then click the **Bullets button** 🔲 on the Formatting toolbar

   Bullet characters appear in front of each item in the list, as shown in Figure 3-11. You can change the bullet characters if you'd like. See the related topic "Bullets and numbers" for more information. To clarify the sequence of the steps in the directions, Angela decides to number the list of directions.

2. Select the four items starting with "Take I-5 ..." at the end of the second paragraph, then click the **Numbering button** 🔲 on the Formatting toolbar

   The list of directions is now a numbered list. Angela realizes that she forgot to include a step in her directions, so she inserts the step in the list.

3. Place the insertion point after step 2 in the list of directions, then press **[Enter]**

   When you press [Enter], the remaining items are renumbered to reflect a new item in the middle of the list. Now Angela can type the additional step.

4. After the number, type **Turn left at lights**

   Next Angela wants the list of directions to match the alignment of the schedule of events. She can do this by changing the indentation of these paragraphs using the Increase Indent button on the Formatting toolbar.

5. Select all the paragraphs in the list of directions, then click the **Increase Indent button** 🔲 on the Formatting toolbar

   The list of directions is indented at the ½" mark. Angela decides that the list of departments should also have the same alignment as the other lists in the document.

6. Select all the paragraphs in the list of departments, then click 🔲

   The list is aligned with the other lists in the document. This completes the formatting for the cover letter. Angela is now ready to save and print her letter.

7. Click the **Save button** 🔲 on the Standard toolbar

8. Click the **Print button** 🔲 to print the entire document

   Compare your document to Figure 3-12. Angela now wants to close the letter then begin formatting the document containing the summary of highlights.

9. Click **File** on the menu bar, then click **Close**

FIGURE 3-11:
Bulleted list

Bullets

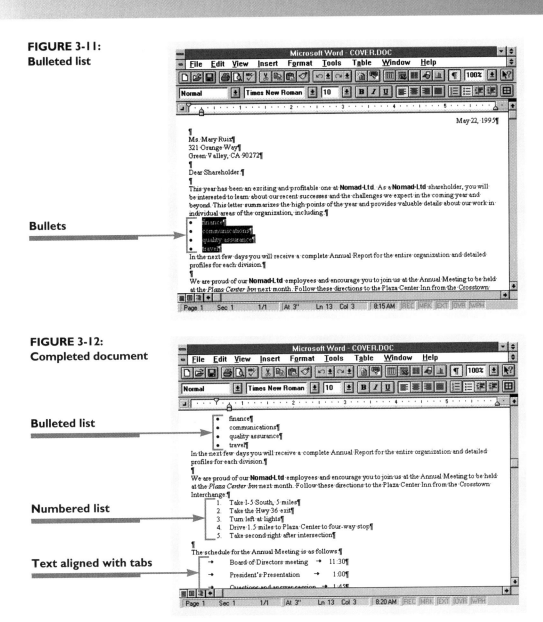

FIGURE 3-12:
Completed document

Bulleted list

Numbered list

Text aligned with tabs

Bullets and numbering options

You can select other number formats or bullet styles by using the Bullets and
Numbering command on the Format menu, which displays the Bullets and
Numbering dialog box shown in Figure 3-13.

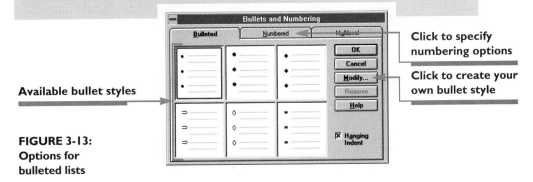

Available bullet styles

Click to specify
numbering options

Click to create your
own bullet style

FIGURE 3-13:
Options for
bulleted lists

Formatting a document with AutoFormat and the Style Gallery

You can have Word automatically format your document with AutoFormat. With this feature, Word makes a number of changes, described in Table 3-4, that improve the appearance of a document. Word also applies a set of styles stored in a template. A **style** is a named set of format settings that you can apply to text. For example, a heading style determines how a title is formatted. A **template** is a special document containing styles and other options you want to use in a specific document. You can also use the Style Gallery to format your document in styles from different templates provided by Word. ▶ Angela wants to add attractive formatting to the summary document. First she'll use the AutoFormat button to apply formatting from the current (and default) template, NORMAL.DOT.

1. **Open the document named UNIT_3-2.DOC from your Student Disk and save it as EXECSUMM.DOC to your MY_FILES directory**
   This document is the summary of the year's highlights at Nomad Ltd.

2. **Click the AutoFormat button** 🖼️ **on the Standard toolbar**
   AutoFormat enhances the appearance of the document, as shown in Figure 3-14. Headings now appear in a larger, bold Arial font. Bullets replace hyphens in the list, and the ™ symbol replaces (tm). The document looks much better, but Angela decides to give it a more contemporary "feel" by choosing a different template from the Style Gallery.

3. **Click Format on the menu bar, then click Style Gallery**
   The Style Gallery dialog box opens, as shown in Figure 3-15. In this dialog box, you can choose from the list of templates that Word provides, and preview your document as it would appear formatted with styles from the selected template. Angela selects a contemporary template and previews the document.

4. **In the Template list box, scroll the list of templates, then click REPORT2**
   In the Preview of box, the document appears as it would if formatted with the styles in the REPORT2 template. Angela decides to format the document using the styles in this template.

5. **Click OK**
   Word applies the styles defined in the template to your document. Compare your document to Figure 3-16. Note that the text in the body of the document changes to Arial, the headings for each topic appear in all uppercase, and a line appears under each heading. To see which style was applied to the headings, Angela places the insertion point in a heading.

6. **Place the insertion point in the heading Balancing the Books and notice the style name that appears in the Style list box on the Formatting toolbar**
   The style name Heading 1 in the Style list box indicates this is the style applied to the current paragraph. Because of its location under the large bold title, the text "Milestones" was not correctly analyzed as a heading during the AutoFormat process. It should be formatted the same as the other headings. Angela can quickly apply the Heading 1 style to this text.

7. **Place the insertion point in the heading Milestones, then click the Style list arrow on the Formatting toolbar**
   The Style list box displays the styles available in the REPORT2 template. Angela selects Heading 1 because this is the style that AutoFormat applied to the other headings in the document.

8. **Scroll through the Style list box, then click Heading 1**

9. **Click the Save button** 🖫 **on the Standard toolbar**

FIGURE 3-14:
Document formatted
with AutoFormat

Bullets replace hyphens

New formatting for
headings

Symbol replaces (tm)

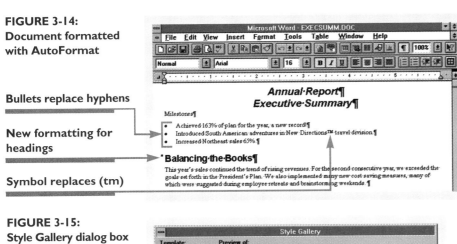

FIGURE 3-15:
Style Gallery dialog box

Default **NORMAL.DOT**
is current

Available templates

Example of current
document in current
template styles

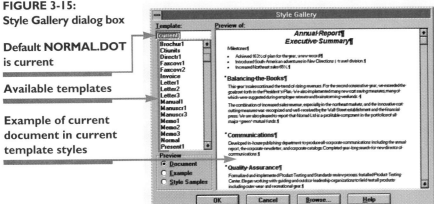

FIGURE 3-16:
Reformatted document
with REPORT2 styles

New heading style

Line

New body text style

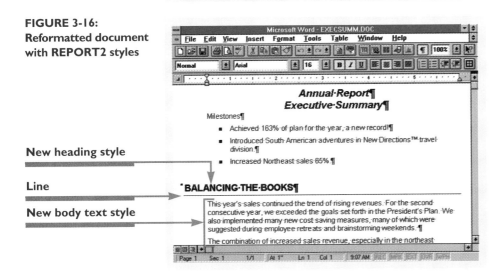

QUICK **TIP**

To review the changes
made with AutoFormat,
use the AutoFormat
command on the
Format menu (instead
of the AutoFormat
button). Then in the
AutoFormat dialog box,
click Review Changes
to examine and then
reject or accept indi-
vidual changes.■

TABLE 3-4: Changes made by AutoFormat

CHANGE	DESCRIPTION
Applies styles	Applies paragraph styles to all paragraphs in a document, including headings, lists, body text, salutations, addresses, etc.
Adjusts spacing	Adds and removes extra paragraph marks as needed; replaces spaces and tabs with proper indentation
Replaces symbols and characters	Replaces hyphens and other symbols used to denote a list with bullets; replaces "straight" quotes with "Smart" (curly) quotes; inserts the trademark, registered trademark, and copyright symbols where indicated

Modifying styles

When you use styles to format text, you can change format settings quickly and consistently for every occurrence of the style in the document. By modifying a style, the appearance of all text formatted in that style also changes. You save time and make fewer mistakes because you don't need to search for each occurrence of text that has formatting you want to change. See the related topic "More about styles and templates" for more information. ▶ After reviewing the new formatting, Angela decides that the headings formatted in all uppercase look too big in the document. After modifying the case format (with the Change Case command) for the first heading, she'll update the Heading 1 style to change all the text formatted with this style.

1 Select the heading **MILESTONES** at the beginning of the document

2 Click **Format** on the menu bar, then click **Change Case**
The Change Case dialog box opens. In this dialog box, you can specify the case—uppercase or lowercase—for selected text. Angela wants the text to appear with only the first character of each word in uppercase, so she decides to use the format called Title Case.

3 Click the **Title Case radio button**, then click **OK**
The selected text appears with the first character of each word capitalized. Now that this heading contains the formatting she prefers, Angela needs to modify the Heading 1 style based on the modified "Milestones" heading to format all the headings in the document in the same way.

4 With the text still selected, click the **Style list arrow** on the Formatting toolbar, then click **Heading 1**
The Reapply Style dialog box opens, as shown in Figure 3-17. You can either redefine the style based on the selected text, or reformat the selected text with the original attributes of the style. In this case, Angela wants to modify the style based on the currently selected text.

5 Click **OK** to redefine the Heading 1 style based on the currently selected text
All text formatted with the Heading 1 style now appears in the Title Case format throughout the document.

6 Click the **Save button** 🖫 on the Standard toolbar
Compare your document to Figure 3-18.

FIGURE 3-17: Reapply Style dialog box

Redefines style based on selection default

Reapplies previous style formatting to selection

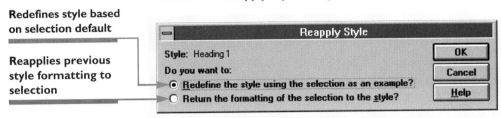

FIGURE 3-18: Updated style

Updated Heading 1 style

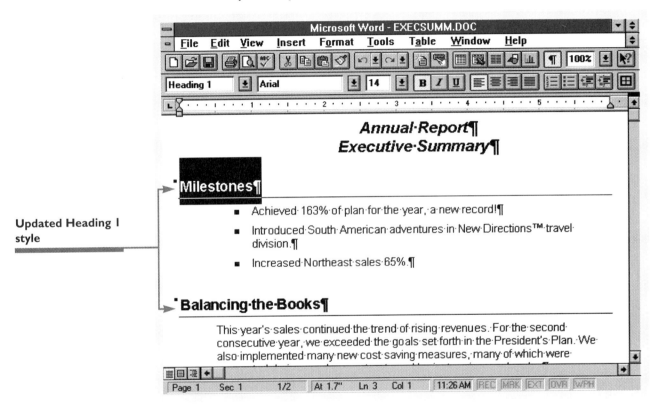

More about styles and templates

A **paragraph style** is a collection of paragraph format settings that affect an entire paragraph (like the styles you used in this lesson). **Character styles** affect only selected text, not entire paragraphs. Character styles are not created with the AutoFormat command, so you must use the Style command on the Format menu to create them. The format settings of a style are determined by a template. For example, in the template called REPORT1, the Body Text style formats text in Times New Roman, whereas in the REPORT2 template, the same style formats text in the Arial font. Word comes with many different templates, each containing collections of styles with a variety of format settings that are appropriate for the kind of document you want to create.

QUICK **TIP**

You can quickly apply a style by pressing [Ctrl][Shift][S], typing the name of the style, then pressing [Enter].

Applying borders and shading

Borders and shading add visual interest to paragraphs of text. **Borders** are lines you can add to the top, bottom, or sides of paragraphs. Preset border settings make it easy to create a box around a paragraph. You can also select lines of varying thickness, including double lines. **Shading** is a background color or pattern you add behind the text of a paragraph. You can apply both borders and shading to emphasize areas of your document. ▶ Angela wants to use borders and shading to emphasize certain areas in the document. First, she'll add a shadow box around the text in the title to set it off from the rest of the document.

1 Select the first two lines of the document, click **Format** on the menu bar, then click **Borders and Shading**
   The Paragraph Borders and Shading dialog box opens, as shown in Figure 3-19. Make sure the Borders tab is selected. The Border section of the dialog box gives you a preview of the border settings you make for your document.

2 In the Presets section, click the **Shadow icon**
   This selection creates a shadow box around the selected paragraphs. A shadow box has thicker lines on the right and bottom, creating a shadow effect for the box. Angela decides to specify a thicker line for the box. Note that like fonts, line thickness is measured in points (pts).

3 In the Style section, click **1½ pt** then click **OK**
   The dialog box closes and the text you selected is formatted with a shadow box border with a 1½ pt line. Note that the border extends to the left and right margins. Next, Angela wants to add shading behind the three lines of text describing Nomad's milestones. This time she'll use the Borders toolbar to format the text.

4 Click the **Borders button** ⊞ on the Formatting toolbar
   The Borders toolbar appears at the top of the document window, as shown in Figure 3-20. The Borders toolbar contains many of the same settings available in the Paragraph Borders and Shading dialog box.

5 Select the three lines of text below the **Milestones** heading, then click the **Shading list arrow**
   Angela wants to emphasize this text by applying a light gray background to it.

6 Click **10%**
   The text appears with a shaded background.

7 Click ⊞ on the Formatting toolbar, then deselect the text
   The Borders toolbar is no longer displayed. Compare your document to Figure 3-21.

8 Click the **Save button** 🖫 on the Standard toolbar

FIGURE 3-19: Paragraph Borders and Shading dialog box

Creates box borders

Display border settings

Available line styles
and thickness options

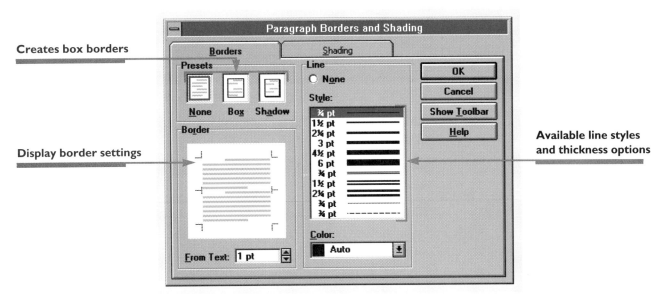

FIGURE 3-20: Borders toolbar

Click to display line
style and thickness
options

Border buttons affect
part of paragraph with
border

Shading options affect
background shading

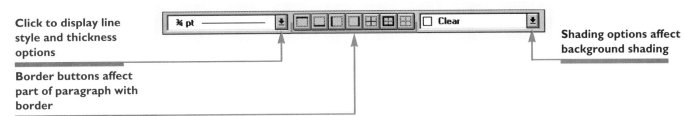

FIGURE 3-21: Borders and shading in the document

Shadow box border
applied

Shading applied

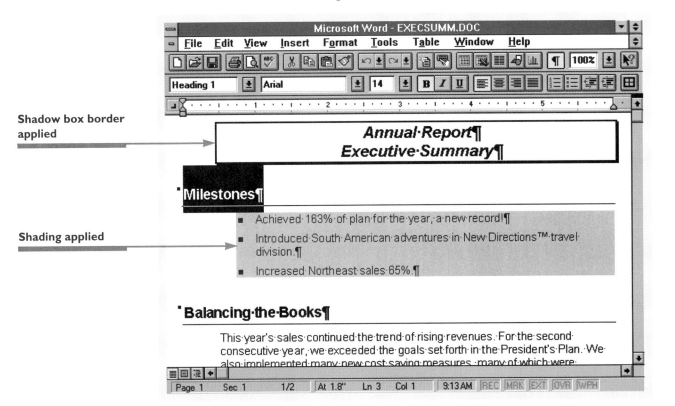

Formatting a paragraph with a drop cap

Another way to draw attention to a specific part of a document is to use a drop cap. A **drop cap** is the first letter of a paragraph that is formatted to be dramatically larger than the rest of the text in the paragraph. This kind of formatting is often used in newsletters, magazines, and newspapers. In Word, you can use the Drop Cap command on the Format menu to create this visually interesting effect in your own documents. ▶ To highlight the importance of the last paragraph in the document, Angela decides to use a drop cap.

1   Place the insertion point in the last paragraph of the document
    You do not need to select the character you want formatted as a drop cap.

2   Click **Format** on the menu bar, then click **Drop Cap**
    The Drop Cap dialog box opens, as shown in Figure 3-22. In this dialog box, you can specify how you want the drop cap formatted. For example, using the custom options you can specify a different font for the drop cap, the number of lines to drop the letter, and the distance from the drop cap to the rest of the paragraph. Angela wants to use the Dropped format and extend the drop cap to two lines.

3   In the Position section, click the **Dropped icon**, type **2** in the Lines to Drop text box, then click **OK**
    A message box appears informing you that using drop caps formats the text with a frame and that to see the text formatted with a frame, you need to display the document in page layout view. See Table 3-5 for a summary of the different document views, and read the related topics "Displaying document views" for more information.

4   Click **Yes** in the message box to display the document in page layout view
    The first character of the paragraph is now two times larger than the surrounding text, as shown in Figure 3-23. Note that a frame appears around the drop cap and the text of the paragraph is formatted around the drop cap. You will learn about using frames in the next unit. For now, Angela wants to add even greater emphasis to this paragraph, so she formats the drop cap in bold.

5   Select the letter **N** inside the frame, click the **Bold button** **B** on the Formatting toolbar, then click outside of the drop cap to deselect the text
    To distinguish the general nature of the mission statement from the specific information about each department in the document, Angela centers the heading for the mission statement.

6   Select the heading **Corporate Mission Statement**, click the **Center button** on the Formatting toolbar, then deselect the text
    Angela has completed formatting the text for now, so she previews the document to see how it will look when she prints it.

7   Click the **Print Preview button** on the Standard toolbar to display the document in print preview

8   Click the **Multiple Pages button** to display both pages of the document, if necessary
    The Multiple Pages button allows you to specify the number of pages of your document you want to display in print preview. To select multiple pages, hold down the Multiple Pages button and drag to select the number of pages you want to see.

9   Click the **Close button** on the Print Preview toolbar to return to your document, then click the **Save button** on the Standard toolbar
    You'll continue working in page layout view to make final changes, then print the document.

FIGURE 3-22: Drop Cap dialog box

Drop cap styles

Custom options

FIGURE 3-23:
Drop cap in the
document

Drop cap

Frame around drop cap

Outline View

Page Layout View

Normal View

View buttons

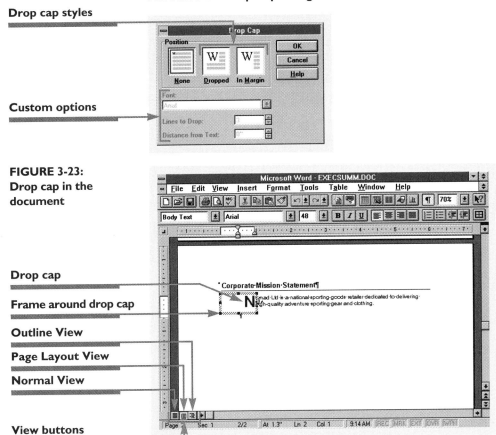

Displaying document views

The different document views allow you to focus on different aspects of word processing. For example, to see the arrangement of text in columns or frames and still be able to edit the document, you need to display the document in page layout view. You can quickly switch views by clicking the view buttons on the left of the horizontal scroll bar, as shown in Figure 3-23. Additional views (described in Table 3-5) are available on the View menu, the File menu, and the Standard toolbar.

TABLE 3-5: Document views

VIEW	DESCRIPTION	USE TO
Normal	Displays the default document view	Type, format, and edit text. You cannot see text arranged with special formatting such as drop caps, frames, or columns in normal view.
Page layout	Displays the document as it will appear when printed	Edit and view placement of text and graphics on the page as it will appear when printed. You see the edges of the page, as well as headers and footers in the document.
Outline	Displays selected level of headings and body text	View major headings to easily reorganize a large document. Your documents need to have Heading styles applied before you can use outline view effectively.
Print preview	Displays entire page(s) on one screen	Review page breaks, all pages, and formatting, and make minor changes to text before printing.

Adjusting document margins

A **margin** is the distance between the text of a document and the top, bottom, or side edges of the page. With the Page Setup command, you can change the amount of space that surrounds the text. You can individually adjust the top, bottom, left, and right margins. You might decide to change the margins to fit more (or less) text on a page, add extra space next to text for notes, or simply create an interesting effect by using white space. **White space** is the part of a page that contains no text. ▶ When she previewed the document, Angela noticed that a small part of the document appears on a page by itself. She decides to adjust the margins so that the document will fit on one page.

I Click **File** on the menu bar, then click **Page Setup**
The Page Setup dialog box opens, as shown in Figure 3-24. In the dialog box, you have a variety of options that affect the appearance of the overall pages of text. Angela wants to adjust the page margins, so she will use the options on the Margins tab.

2 Click the **Margins tab**, if it is not already selected in the dialog box
To change the margin settings, you can either click the up and down arrows next to the appropriate box, or type the setting you want in the box. Angela wants to reduce the top margin to 0.5".

3 Click the **Top down arrow** until it displays **0.5"**
This setting will reduce the amount of space at the top of the page from 1" to ½". The Preview section shows the effect of this change in the document. Generally, the bottom margin should be the same size as the top margin, so Angela needs to adjust the bottom margin as well.

4 Click the **Bottom down arrow** until it displays **0.5"**
This setting will reduce the amount of space at the bottom of the page from 1" to ½". To allow even more room for text on the page, Angela decides to reduce the space at the left and right margins.

5 Click the **Left down arrow** until it displays **I"**
This setting will reduce the amount of space at the left of the page from 1.25" to 1". Angela needs to adjust the right margin to match the left margin.

6 Click the **Right down arrow** until it displays **I"** then click **OK**
Angela has finished adjusting the margins and is now ready to save and preview her document.

7 Click the **Save button** 🖫 on the Standard toolbar, then click the **Print Preview button** 🔍 to display the document in print preview
The document appears on one page. Compare your document to Figure 3-25. Angela now wants to print the document then exit Word.

8 Click the **Print button** 🖨 on the Print Preview toolbar

9 Click **File** on the menu bar, then click **Exit**
If a dialog box appears asking if you want to save changes to NORMAL.DOT (the default template), click No. This prevents you from changing to the default styles in NORMAL.DOT. Changing NORMAL.DOT can affect format settings and styles for other Word users on your computer.

FIGURE 3-24: Page Setup dialog box

Adjusts distance
between text and
edge of page

Represents current
margin settings

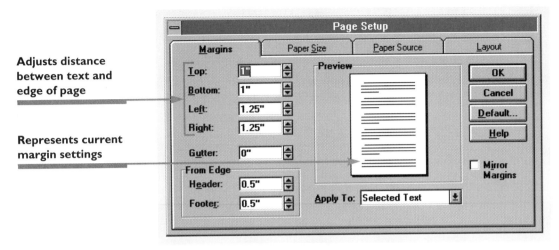

FIGURE 3-25: Document in print preview

Document now fits on
one page

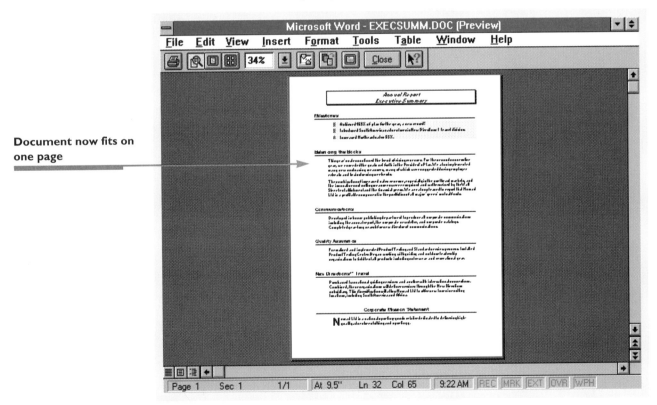

CONCEPTSREVIEW

Label each of the formatting elements used in the document shown in Figure 3-26.

1 _____

2 _____

3 _____

4 _____

5 _____

6 _____

7 _____

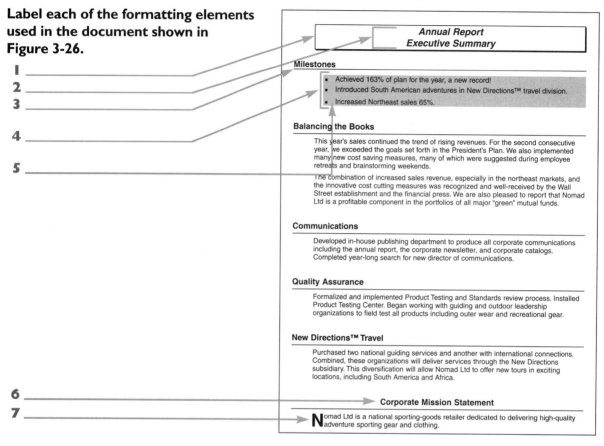

FIGURE 3-26

Match each of the following terms with the statement that best describes its function.

8 Changes the appearance of letters, numbers, and punctuation

9 A named set of paragraph format settings

10 Symbols or graphics preceding items in a list

11 Lines added to paragraphs of text

12 Changes the line spacing, alignment, and space between paragraphs

13 Displays documents in alternative collections of styles

14 Collections of styles

15 Changes the first character of a paragraph to be significantly larger than the surrounding text

a. Bullets

b. Borders

c. Paragraph styles

d. Text formatting

e. Templates

f. Style Gallery

g. Paragraph formatting

h. Drop cap

Select the best answer from the list of choices:

16 Which text formatting feature is NOT available on the Formatting toolbar?

  a. Bold

  b. Italics

  c. Double-underline

  d. Character styles

17 Which paragraph formatting feature is NOT available on the Formatting toolbar?

  a. Paragraph alignment

  b. Line spacing

  c. Paragraph styles

  d. Indentation

18 To add a specific amount of space between paragraphs, the best solution is to

  a. Press [Enter] until you get the amount of space you want

  b. Use the Spacing Before and After options in the Paragraph dialog box

c. Adjust the top margin for each paragraph

d. Use the Line Spacing options in the Paragraph dialog box

19 Which command automatically formats the first character of a paragraph to be significantly larger than the rest of the text in the paragraph?

a. The Change Case command on the Format menu

b. The Font command on the Format menu

c. The Drop Cap command on the Format menu

d. The Drop Cap button on the Formatting toolbar

20 Which of the following is the fastest way to change from all uppercase to all lowercase?

a. The Change Case command on the Format menu

b. The Font command on the Format menu

c. The Drop Cap command on the Format menu

d. The Font Size button on the Formatting toolbar

APPLICATIONSREVIEW

1 Format text.

a. Start Word and open the document named UNIT_3-3.DOC from your Student Disk. Save the document as OPENROAD.DOC to your MY_FILES directory.

b. Select the first occurrence of "OpenRoads(tm), Inc." then click the Bold button on the Formatting toolbar. With the text still selected, click the Italic button.

c. Use the Format Painter to apply this formatting to the second occurrence of this name in the document.

d. Save your changes.

2 Create bulleted lists.

a. Select the list of items starting with "tracks the location..." and ending with "generates pre-printed..."

b. Click the Bullets button on the Formatting toolbar, then click to deselect the text.

c. Select the two items "1-5 lb. shipment" and "5-10 lb. shipment" and make these bulleted items also.

3 Use AutoFormat.

a. Click the AutoFormat button to apply standard styles and formatting to your document.

b. Review the changes in your document.

4 Use the Style Gallery.

a. Click Format on the menu bar, then click Style Gallery.

b. Select several different templates and examine your document as it would appear formatted in these templates.

c. Click Letter2 in the list of templates, then click OK.

d. Save your changes.

5 Apply paragraph formatting and styles.

a. With the insertion point in the first paragraph in the body of the letter, click the Justify button on the Formatting toolbar.

b. Select the Body Text style from the Style list box.

c. Make sure the option for redefining the style is selected in the Reapply Style dialog box, then click OK.

d. Save your changes.

6 Adjust page margins.

a. Click File on the menu bar, then click Page Setup. Make sure the Margins tab is displayed in the Page Setup dialog box.

b. In the Top text box, specify a 2" margin.

c. In the Bottom text box, specify a 2" margin.

d. In the Left text box, specify a 1.5" margin.

e. In the Right text box, specify a 1.5" margin.

f. Save your changes.

g. Be sure to select the placeholder [your name] at the bottom of the letter and replace it with your name.

h. Preview then print your document. Your completed document should look like Figure 3-27. Exit Word.

Mr. Steven Wing
1290 Industrial Boulevard
Suite 8B
Eagle Ridge, OR 09005

Dear Mr. Wing:

Thank you for taking the time to complete the customer survey for *Open Roads™, Inc.* As promised, I have enclosed a demonstration copy of our new package tracking software, RoadMap™. This useful application provides the following capabilities:

- tracks the location and delivery times of all your packages worldwide
- provides total shipping weight and price
- generates pre-printed air bills and labels

With a personal computer, a modem, and RoadMap™ software from *Open Roads™, Inc.* you can have this useful feature at your fingertips. If you decide to purchase this software, you can receive substantial savings on our shipping services:

- 1-5 lb. shipment
- 5-10 lb. shipment

I will contact you next week to answer any questions you have.

Sincerely,

[your name]
Open Roads, Inc.
Account Representative

FIGURE 3-27

INDEPENDENT
CHALLENGE 1

Suppose you are in charge of marketing for a community orchestra. As part of your responsibilities, you must prepare a poster for an upcoming concert series. Your assistant has already prepared a draft for you, and you need to format it to improve its appearance. Open the document named UNIT_3-4.DOC from your Student Disk and save it as MUSCNITE.DOC to your MY_FILES directory. Start your formatting by using the AutoFormat button. Then use Figure 3-28 as a guide for further enhancing the document's appearance. When finished formatting, preview then print your document.

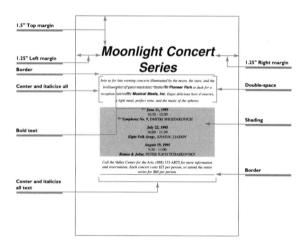

FIGURE 3-28

INDEPENDENT
CHALLENGE 2

You are the director of communications for a small software company, MySoft International. Your task is to prepare for the release of a new multimedia educational game called "CrazyBugz." This package, designed for children 8 to 14 years old, allows the creative assembly of a variety of eight-legged creatures, real and imaginary, using computer software. Open the document named UNIT_3-5.DOC from your Student Disk and save it as CRZYBUGZ.DOC to your MY_FILES directory. First improve the appearance of the document using AutoFormat, then create a press release based on the PRESREL2 template in the Style Gallery. Apply the Title style to the centered text. Then use Figure 3-29 as a guide for further enhancing the document's appearance. Be sure to replace the placeholder [Your Name] with your name. When finished formatting, preview then print your document. Close the document then exit Word.

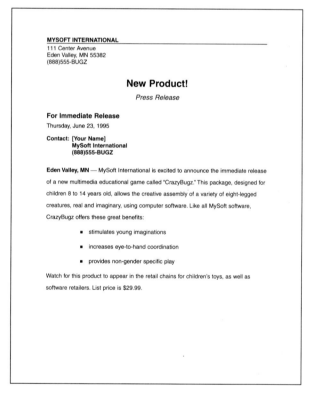

FIGURE 3-29

UNIT 4

OBJECTIVES

- ▶ Create a table
- ▶ Add rows and columns in a table
- ▶ Calculate data in a table
- ▶ Format a table
- ▶ Arrange text in columns
- ▶ Position text using frames
- ▶ Insert and position graphics
- ▶ Create headers and footers

Arranging
TEXT AND GRAPHICS

By formatting text and paragraphs, you can make your document easier to read. Word provides additional formatting techniques for arranging text and graphics on the page to give your document a polished, professional appearance. For example, by formatting text in a table you can quickly add or delete text without reformatting all the rows and columns, and you can use the Table AutoFormat command to make a table easier to read with preset borders and shading combinations. By adding and positioning graphics in a document, you can achieve dramatic effects. ▶ Angela used different formatting techniques to produce a simple report summarizing the year's highlights; now she wants to use the same text in a newsletter format for the Nomad Ltd senior management newsletter, the *Executive Bulletin*. ▶

Creating a table

A **table** is text arranged in a grid of rows and columns. You can use the Insert Table button on the Standard toolbar or the Insert Table command on the Table menu to create a blank table wherever you place the insertion point. The Insert Table button displays a grid (as shown in Figure 4-1) in which you drag to select the number of rows and columns you want; with the Insert Table command you can specify the number of rows and columns and choose different table formatting options. ▶ Angela wants the *Executive Bulletin* newsletter to display financial information about company profits in a table.

1 Start Word and insert your Student Disk in drive A
Refer to the "Word 6.0 Screen Check" section on the "Read This Before You Begin Microsoft Word 6.0" page to make sure your Word screen is set up appropriately.

2 Open the document named UNIT_4-1.DOC from your Student Disk and save it as BULLETIN.DOC to your MY_FILES directory
This document is similar to the one you used in the previous unit; however, it contains additional text about a new department and additional formatting.

3 Place the insertion point in front of the second paragraph mark below the last item in the list of Milestones, then click the **Insert Table button** 🔳 on the Standard toolbar
Angela's table requires four columns (one for each of the years, plus one for the divisions) and five rows (one for each of the divisions, plus one for the columns headings).

4 Drag in the grid until it indicates a **5 x 4 Table**, then release the mouse button
A grid of cells appears, as shown in Figure 4-2. A **cell** is the intersection of a row and a column, and contains a **cell marker** identifying the end of the contents in the cell. The **end-of-row marker** outside the table identifies the end of a row. **Gridlines** surround each cell so that you can see the structure of the table. Neither the markers nor gridlines appear when you print the document. Now that Angela has created the structure for her table, she can enter the column headings.

5 With the insertion point in the first cell, type **Division** then press **[Tab]**
To move to the next cell in a table, press [Tab]. To move to the previous cell, press [Shift][Tab]. Angela can now enter the headings for the three remaining columns. To show company profits for the past three *fiscal years*, she uses the designation "FY."

6 Type the following text in the remaining cells in the first row; be sure to press **[Tab]** to move to the next cell:
FY 1994   FY 1993   FY 1992   [Tab]

7 Type the remaining information, as shown in Figure 4-3, pressing **[Tab]** to move to the next cell; do *not* press [Tab] at the end of the last row

8 Click the **Save button** 💾 on the Standard toolbar
Your changes are saved in the document. Compare your document to Figure 4-3.

FIGURE 4-1:
Specifying rows and columns with the Insert Table button

Drag to specify number of rows and columns

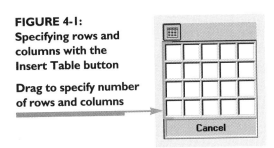

FIGURE 4-2:
New table in the document

Cell

Table

Cell marker

Gridlines

End-of-row markers

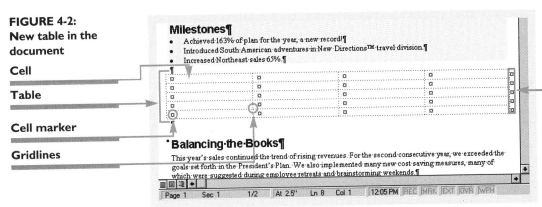

FIGURE 4-3:
Text in the table

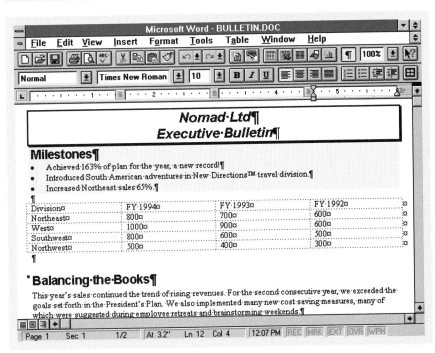

Converting text to a table

You can convert existing text that is already formatted with tabs, commas, or paragraph marks into a table by selecting the text and then using the Insert Table button on the Standard toolbar, or the Insert Table command or the Convert Text to Table command on the Table menu.

TROUBLE?

By default, Word displays gridlines in a table. If the gridlines do not appear in your table, click Table on the menu bar, then click Gridlines.■

Adding rows and columns in a table

When working with tables, you often need to change the number of rows or columns to add or remove information. You can quickly add or delete rows and columns without having to rearrange text in the table. To work with tables you use different navigation keys. Table 4-1 summarizes how to move around and select text in a table. ▶ Angela would like to include total figures for each division for the last three years. She also wants to provide totals for the entire company in each year. So that she can include these calculations, Angela needs to add one row and one column to the table.

1 Place the insertion point in the last cell of the last row of the table (if it is not already there), then press **[Tab]**
Pressing [Tab] in the last cell of the last row creates a new row of cells at the bottom of the table. The insertion point is in the first cell of the new row, so Angela can type a label.

2 Type **Nomad Ltd**
Next, Angela will add a new column to the end of the table. To do so, she must first select the end-of-row markers at the right edge of the table.

3 At the top-right edge of the table, position the pointer above the end-of-row marker, and when the pointer changes to ↓, as shown in Figure 4-4, click the **left mouse button**
The column of end-of-row markers is selected, as shown in Figure 4-4. With the end-of-row markers selected, Angela can now add another column to the table.

See the related topic "Using the selection bar in tables" for more information on selection techniques.

4 Click **Table** on the menu bar, then click **Insert Columns**
A new blank column is inserted at the right end of the table, beyond the document margins. You might need to scroll your window to the right to see the new column. (You will learn to adjust column widths later in this unit.) You can also click the Insert Columns/Rows button ▦ on the Standard toolbar to insert a new column or row. This button is the same as the Insert Table button, but the ToolTip name for the button changes based on what is currently selected.

5 Click to place the insertion point in the first cell of the new column, then type **Total**
The column is no longer selected, and the text appears at the top of the column.

6 Place the insertion point in the first cell under the Total column heading to prepare for the next lesson

7 Click the **Save button** ▦ on the Standard toolbar to save your changes

FIGURE 4-4:
Selecting a column

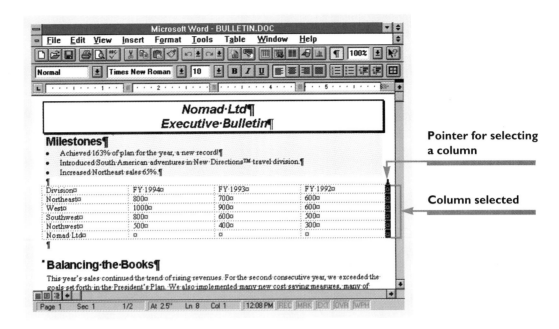

Pointer for selecting a column

Column selected

Using the selection bar in tables

The area to the left of each row in a table contains the selection bar. Clicking in the selection bar to the left of a row selects that row in the same way clicking in the selection bar to the left of a line of text selects the entire line. In addition, each cell in the table contains its own selection bar. You can click the selection bar to the left of text in a cell to select an individual cell.

TABLE 4-1: Table navigation and selection techniques

TO	PRESS
Move to and select the contents of the next cell in a table	[Tab]
Move to and select the contents of the previous cell in a table	[Shift][Tab]
Move to the first cell in a row	[Alt][Home]
Move to the last cell in a row	[Alt][End]
Move to the top cell in a column	[Alt][Page Up]
Move to the bottom cell in a column	[Alt][Page Down]
Select a column	[Alt] and click the left mouse button
Select the entire table	[Alt][5] on the numeric keypad ([Num Lock] must be turned off)

QUICK **TIP**

To quickly delete a row or column using the keyboard, select the row or column then press [Shift][Delete] or [Ctrl][X]. To remove only the text from a selected row or column, press [Delete].■

Calculating data in a table

With the Formula command, you can perform calculations on the data in a table. Built-in formulas make it easy to quickly perform standard calculations (such as totals or averages), or you can enter your own formulas. See the related topic "Creating your own calculations" for more information. ▶ In the new column and row Angela added, she'll use the Formula command to calculate the totals she needs.

1 Click **Table** on the menu bar, then click **Formula**
The Formula dialog box opens, as shown in Figure 4-5. In this dialog box, you can select a built-in formula or specify your own. Based on the location of the insertion point in the table, Word suggests a formula in the Formula box—in this case, the built-in SUM formula—and suggests which cells to use in the calculation. In this case, the values in the cells to the *left* of the insertion point will be added and displayed as the total. This is the formula that Angela wants.

2 Click **OK**
The dialog box closes and the sum of the values in the row appears in the current cell. To repeat this calculation for the other totals, Angela presses [F4] in each row. The F4 key repeats your last action.

3 Press **[↓]** to move the insertion point to the next cell in the Total column, press **[F4]**, then repeat this step in each of the next two cells in this column
The sum of the values in each row appears in each cell in the Total column. Now Angela wants to add the values in each column to determine totals for each year.

4 Place the insertion point in the last cell of the second column, click **Table** on the menu bar, then click **Formula**
The Formula dialog box opens and displays the suggested formula, =SUM(ABOVE). Because this is the formula she wants to use, Angela accepts the default calculation.

5 Click **OK**
The dialog box closes and the sum of the values in the column appears in the current cell. To repeat this calculation for the other totals, Angela presses [F4] in each column.

6 Press **[Tab]** to move to the next column, press **[F4]**, then repeat this step for the two remaining columns
The total amounts appear in the cells for each column. Angela realizes that the number for the Northwest division for 1994 should be 625, not 500. After revising this figure, Angela needs to update the calculations in the table.

7 Select the contents of the second cell in the fifth row (500), then type **625**
The new value appears in the cell. However, Word does not automatically update the totals to reflect the new value. Angela needs to recalculate the totals in the table using [F9].

8 With the insertion point somewhere in the table, click **Table** on the menu bar, click **Select Table**, then press **[F9]**
Click anywhere outside of the table to deselect it. Note that the totals in the table are updated to reflect the new value. Scroll your window to the right and compare your table to Figure 4-6.

9 Click the **Save button** 🖫 on the Standard toolbar to save your changes

FIGURE 4-5:
Formula dialog box
Default formula

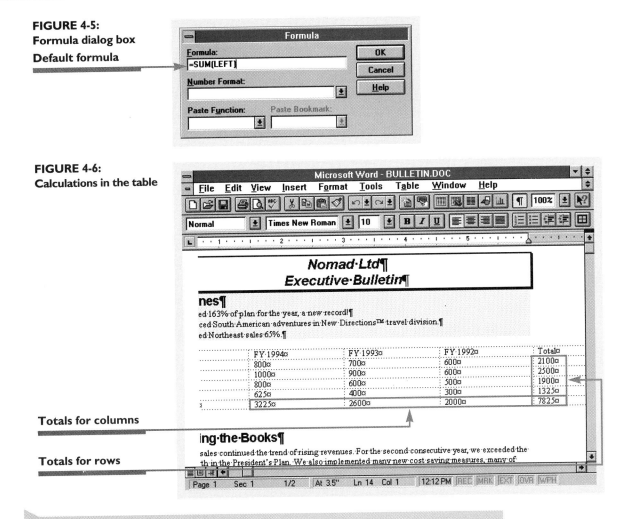

FIGURE 4-6:
Calculations in the table

Totals for columns

Totals for rows

Creating your own calculations

To enter your own calculation in the Formula dialog box, you must refer to other cells in the table using cell references. A **cell reference** identifies a cell's position in the table. Each cell reference contains a letter to identify its column (A, B, C and so on) and a number (1, 2, 3 and so on) to identify its row. For example, the first cell in the first row is A1; the second cell in the first row is B1, and so on. See Figure 4-7. The formula to determine the difference between 1994 and 1993 results for the Northeast division would be =B2−C2. Multiplication is represented by an asterisk (*); division is represented by a slash (/).

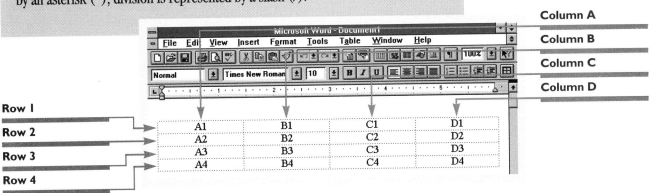

FIGURE 4-7: Cell references

Formatting a table

You can improve the appearance of a table by adding lines and shading. With the Table AutoFormat command you can choose from a variety of preset table formats. ▶ Now that she has entered the financial results in a table and calculated the necessary total amounts, Angela decides to improve the appearance of the table by applying attractive borders and shading using the Table AutoFormat command.

1   **With the insertion point inside the table, click Table on the menu bar, then click Table AutoFormat**
The Table AutoFormat dialog box opens, as shown in Figure 4-8. In this dialog box, you can preview different preset table formats. Angela decides to use a classic preset format.

2   **In the Formats list box, click Classic 4**
The Preview section shows how Classic 4 formats a table. Also, notice that in the Apply Special Format To section, the Heading Rows and First Column options are already selected. This means that special formatting (such as bold text or shading) will be applied to these areas of the table.

3   **Click OK**
Word applies the Classic 4 format to the table. The column headings appear in a white, italicized font on a gray background, and the text in the first column is bold. Because Angela wants the table to span the width of the page, she needs to increase the width of the columns in the table. She can change the size of all the columns with the Cell Height and Width command.

4   **Select the entire table, click Table on the menu bar, then click Cell Height and Width**
The Cell Height and Width dialog box opens. In this dialog box, you can specify the height and width of selected rows and columns.

5   **Click the Column tab**
On the Column tab you can specify the width of selected columns. The width of the document between the left and right margins is approximately 6"; therefore, each column must be 1.2" wide to span the width of the text. With the entire table selected, Angela can change the width of all the columns at once.

6   **Click the Width of Columns up arrow until 1.2" is displayed, then click OK**
The dialog box closes and the table is formatted with columns that span the width of the margins. Angela thinks the table would look better if the contents of columns 2 through 5 were right-aligned.

7   **Select columns 2 through 5 then click the Align Right button ▦ on the Formatting toolbar**
Deselect the table to see that the numbers appear right-aligned in the columns, as shown in Figure 4-9.

8   **Click the Save button ▣ on the Standard toolbar to save your changes**

FIGURE 4-8: Table AutoFormat dialog box

Displays sample table
with new formats

Preset table formats

Highlights parts of a
table with special
formatting

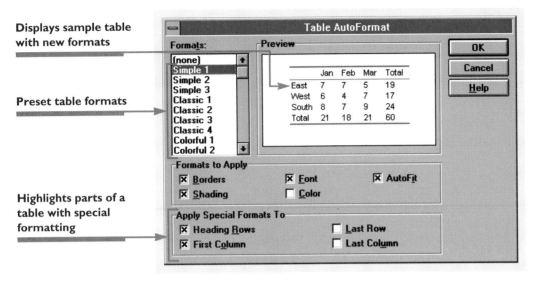

FIGURE 4-9: Completed table

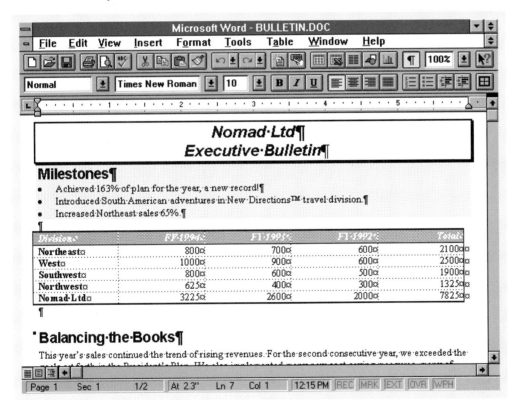

Arranging text in columns

**Creating and
Formatting Sections**

In newsletters, magazines, and other forms of mass communication, it is common to format text in multiple columns rather than in one column as you usually see in letters, reports, and memos. ▶ Angela will explore formatting the document in multiple columns to give the *Executive Bulletin* the appearance of a newsletter. She begins by formatting the document into two columns. She can do this quickly with the Columns button.

1 Press **[Ctrl][Home]** to place the insertion point at the beginning of the document

2 Click the **Columns button** 📖 on the Standard toolbar, then click and drag to select **2 columns**, as shown in Figure 4-10

   Word formats your document into two columns; however, when a document is displayed in normal view, you see only one column. You need to switch to page layout view to display the two columns.

3 Click the **Page Layout View button** 📖 on the horizontal scroll bar

   The document is formatted into two columns, as shown in Figure 4-11. Note that you see only part of the table. To display all of the table, Angela needs to format this part of the document in one column. She can format different parts of the document with different numbers of columns by creating **sections**. She can then format each section individually.

4 With the insertion point in front of the heading **Balancing the Books**, click **Insert** on the menu bar, then click **Break**

   The Break dialog box opens, as shown in Figure 4-12. In this dialog box, you can specify the kind of break you want to insert. Table 4-2 summarizes the types of breaks you can insert in a document.

**TABLE 4-2:
Types of breaks in a
document**

BREAK	DESCRIPTION
Page break	Places the text after the insertion point on a new page; use this break when you want the following text to start on a new page
Column break	Places text after the insertion point in the next column; use this kind of break when you want to redistribute the amount of text that appears in each column
Section break	Creates a new section in the document; use this break when you want to format different parts of the document with different column and page setup settings
Next page section break	Creates a new section on a new page; use this break when you want the next section to start on a new page
Continuous section break	Creates a new section on the same page; use this break when you want the next section to start on the same page
Even page section break	Creates a new section that appears on the next even-numbered page; use this break when you want the next section to start on an even-numbered page
Odd page section break	Creates a new section that appears on the next odd-numbered page; use this break when you want the next section to start on an odd-numbered page

FIGURE 4-10: Specifying columns with the Columns button

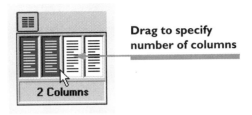

Drag to specify
number of columns

FIGURE 4-11: Columns in page layout view

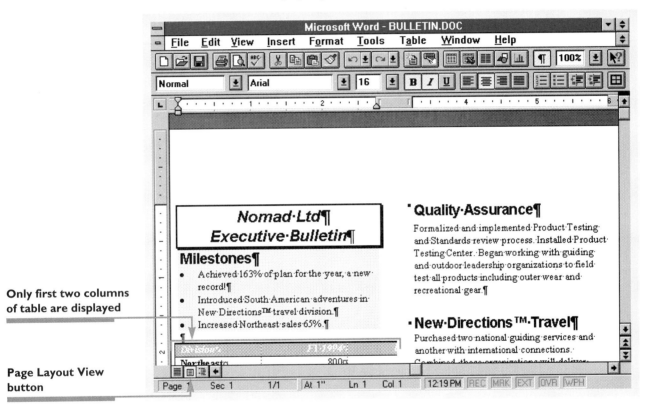

Only first two columns
of table are displayed

Page Layout View
button

FIGURE 4-12: Break dialog box

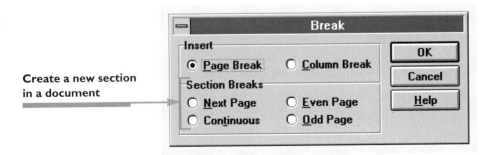

Create a new section
in a document

Arranging text in columns, continued

Because she wants the next section to appear on the same page, Angela selects a continuous section break.

5 In the Section Breaks section, click the **Continuous radio button**, then click **OK**

Word creates a new section that appears on the same page as the previous section. A section break appears as a double-dotted line labeled "End of Section," as shown in Figure 4-13. The status bar now indicates that the insertion point is in section 2. With two sections in her document, Angela can now format the first section as one column, so that the entire width of the table will be visible.

6 Place the insertion point anywhere in section 1 (refer to the status bar for the location), then click ▦ and drag to select **1 column**

The first section, which contains the Milestones information and the table, now appears in one column. To visually balance the formatting at the bottom of the page with the one-column formatting at the top, Angela decides to create another section that will contain the mission statement topic, and format it as one column.

7 Place the insertion point in front of the paragraph mark above the heading **Corporate Mission Statement**, click **Insert** on the menu bar, then click **Break**

In the Break dialog box, Angela again specifies a continuous section break so that the new section appears on the same page.

8 In the Section Breaks section, click the **Continuous radio button**, then click **OK**

With a new section break inserted in the document, Angela can now format the new section in one column.

9 Click ▦ then drag to select **1 Column**

The third section of the document is formatted in one column, as shown in Figure 4-14. To see the results of her changes better, Angela adjusts the magnification of the text.

10 Click the **Zoom Control list arrow** on the right end of the Standard toolbar

The Zoom Control box displays a list of preset magnifications you can use to display your document. With the Zoom Control settings you can increase the magnification to get a close-up view of the text, or you can decrease the magnification to see the overall appearance of a page.

11 Click **Page Width**

The document appears reduced so that you can see three sides (bottom, right, and left) of the page. This setting provides a better view of the text, but Angela prefers to see more of the document, so she can rearrange text on the page more easily. She reduces the magnification to 60%.

12 Select the percentage in the **Zoom Control box**, type **60**, then press **[Enter]**

Now you can see more of the page, as shown in Figure 4-15. Notice that the magnification settings you use depend on the type of monitor you are using and your personal preferences. If the magnification setting is too small for you to work with, consider using a larger setting.

13 Click the **Save button** 💾 on the Standard toolbar to save your changes

FIGURE 4-13:
New section

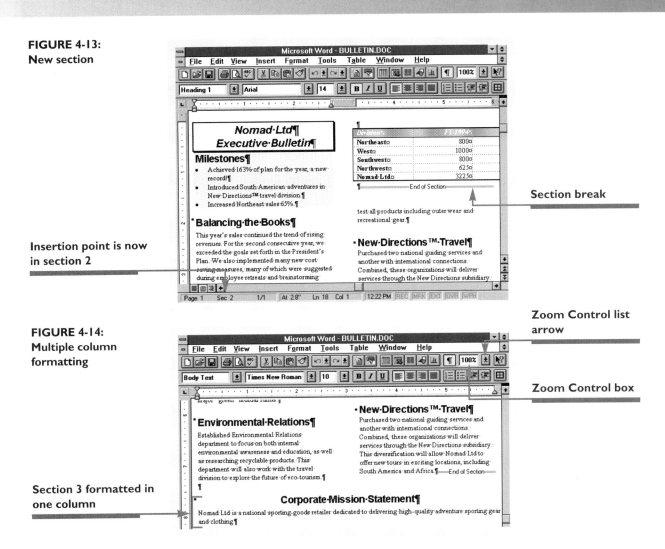

Section break

Insertion point is now
in section 2

Zoom Control list
arrow

FIGURE 4-14:
Multiple column
formatting

Zoom Control box

Section 3 formatted in
one column

FIGURE 4-15:
Document in 60%
magnification

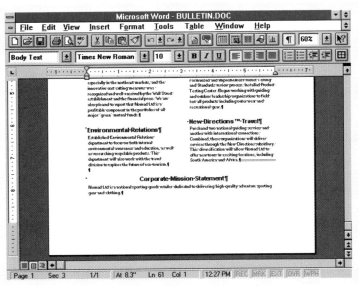

TROUBLE?

Word inserts a break
at the current location
of the insertion point
when you choose the
Break command. If
your formatting is not
what you expected,
you can always click
the Undo button
on the Standard tool-
bar, then verify that
the insertion point is
in the correct location
before you choose
Break.■

Positioning text using frames

Important information can make a greater impact if you adjust the size or position of the area in which the text appears. For example, the shaded text in the first part of the *Executive Bulletin* could be presented attractively as a **sidebar**, which is a smaller boxed section of text positioned vertically next to a main article. To create a sidebar, you need to insert a frame around the appropriate text. As you saw in Unit 3 when creating a drop cap, a **frame** is a border that surrounds text or a graphic so that you can move and format the framed object without affecting the formatting of the surrounding text. With frames you can position text (or graphics) exactly where you want on the page. ▶ Angela decides to position the milestone topics in the left margin to give readers an overview of the topics in the bulletin at a glance.

1 Select the heading **Milestones** and the **three bulleted items** in the list below the heading
   With the text selected, Angela can insert a frame around it.

2 Click **Insert** on the menu bar, then click **Frame**
   A gray hashed border representing the frame appears around the paragraph. Notice that the frame has **handles**—small black boxes— around it; the handles allow you to resize the frame. See the related topic "Dragging sizing handles" for more information. Now Angela can change the size and shape of the area containing the text.

3 Place the pointer over the **right center sizing handle** until the pointer changes to ↔, drag the handle to the left until the frame is about 1.5" wide, then release the mouse button
   The text appears in a long rectangle at the left edge of the page. Framing text gives you a great deal of flexibility in placing the text anywhere you want, even outside the page margins. Notice that an anchor icon appears next to the paragraph containing the framed text. The **anchor icon** indicates the paragraph with which the frame is associated. If you move the paragraph, the framed text moves with it. Next, Angela creates a sidebar by dragging the framed text beyond the left margin.

4 Position the pointer over a border of the frame until the pointer changes to ⊹, then drag the framed text about ½" to the left and about 2½" down so that the anchor icon appears near the Balancing the Books heading
   The sidebar appears outside the left margin as a long box of text. Angela would like the sidebar to be evenly spaced between the beginning and end of the first article.

5 Position the pointer over a border of the frame until the pointer changes to ⊹, and drag the framed text until it is similar to the text shown in Figure 4-16
   Next, Angela makes the text in the sidebar easier to read by using the Arial font.

6 Click the **Font list arrow** on the Formatting toolbar, then click **Arial**
   The text inside the frame appears in the Arial font. Notice that the formatting of the surrounding text is not changed and the right margin has not changed. To improve the appearance of the document, Angela reduces the font size of the items in the bulleted list, which reduces the size of the sidebar.

7 Select the **three bulleted items**, click the **Font Size list arrow** on the Formatting toolbar, then click **9**
   The font size of the bulleted items is reduced without changing the font size of the surrounding text outside the frame. Deselect the text and compare your document to Figure 4-17.

8 Click the **Save button** 🖫 on the Standard toolbar to save your changes

FIGURE 4-16:
Framed and positioned text

Frame border

Anchor icon

Sizing handles

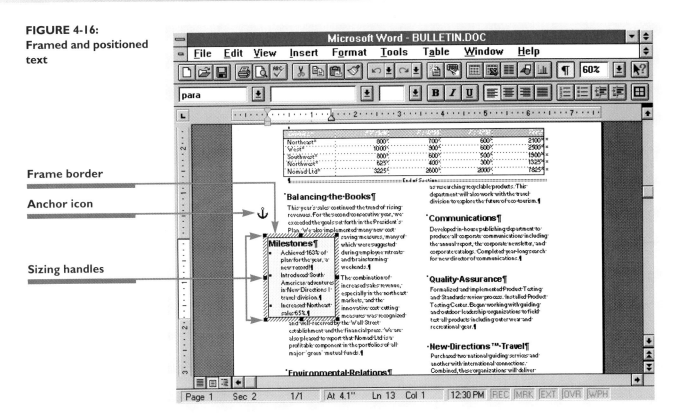

FIGURE 4-17: Formatted and framed text

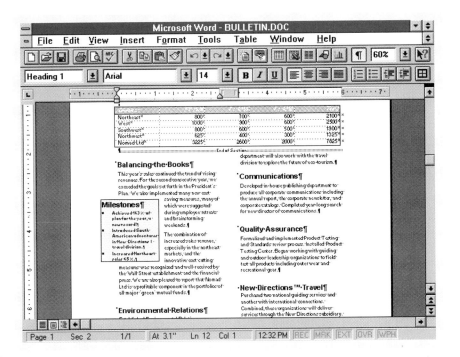

Dragging sizing handles

Dragging a top, bottom, or side handle allows you to size the object in one direction. Dragging a corner handle allows you to size the object in two directions at once, retaining the same proportions.

TROUBLE?

As you move a framed object, the anchor icon might "jump" from line to line. This is normal. After you position the object, you can move it a small amount without changing the position of the anchor icon. This allows you to place the object exactly where you want. Continue moving the object until it appears where you want. Or click the Undo button on the Standard toolbar and place the object again.■

Inserting and positioning graphics

In Word you can insert pictures (in the form of graphic files, many of which are provided with Word) to better illustrate ideas and enhance your document. You can also use graphic files created in other applications. After you insert a graphic, you can size and frame it to fit where you want. ▶ In the *Executive Bulletin*, Angela wants to insert a logo in the article about the new division.

1   Place the insertion point in front of the heading **New Directions™ Travel**, click **Insert** on the menu bar, then click **Picture**
The Insert Picture dialog box opens, as shown in Figure 4-18. In this dialog box, you can select and preview a picture you want to insert in a document. The dialog box displays the default CLIPART directory in the Word directory.

2   In the File Name list box, scroll to and click **COMPASS.WMF**, then click the **Preview Picture check box** (if it is not already selected)
This is the correct graphic the new division is using, so Angela inserts it in the document.

3   Click **OK**
The graphic is inserted in the document at the insertion point. Depending on the type of computer you are using, the graphic might require a moment or two to appear. After inserting a graphic, you often need to resize it using the sizing handles. As you drag a sizing handle, the status bar displays the percentage of change in size. Because the graphic is too large to appear next to the text in the column, Angela drags a corner sizing handle to make the graphic smaller.

4   Select the graphic (if it is not already selected), then drag the sizing handle in the lower-right corner up and to the left until the status bar indicates the graphic is **50%** of its original height and width
The graphic is now smaller, as shown in Figure 4-19. Angela inserts a frame around the graphic to position it below the heading, so that the text in the article surrounds the graphic.

5   Click **Insert** on the menu bar, then click **Frame**

6   Position the graphic down and to the right so that it appears below the New Directions™ Travel heading
The text in the article surrounds the graphic, as shown in Figure 4-20. If the graphic does not look like the one in Figure 4-20, keep positioning it until it does. Next, Angela decides to add a graphic that will serve as a border between the second and third sections in the document.

7   With the insertion point in front of the heading **Corporate Mission Statement**, repeat Steps 1 through 3 to insert the graphic named **TRAVEL.WMF** or if not available, insert any other border-like picture
After inserting the graphic, Angela decides to reduce the height of the graphic by 50% so that it creates a narrower divider between sections.

8   Select the graphic (if necessary) then drag the bottom center sizing handle up until the graphic is **50%** of its original height
The image is distorted a little from the original because it was sized in only one direction. Nevertheless, this is still a pleasing visual effect. Compare your document to Figure 4-21. Note that if you didn't use TRAVEL.WMF, your document will look different.

9   Click the **Save button** 🖫 on the Standard toolbar to save your changes

FIGURE 4-18:
Insert Picture dialog box

Picture files

Default graphics directory

Displays preview of selected graphic

Click to display preview of graphic

FIGURE 4-19:
Sized graphic

Dimensions displayed in status bar

Sizing pointer

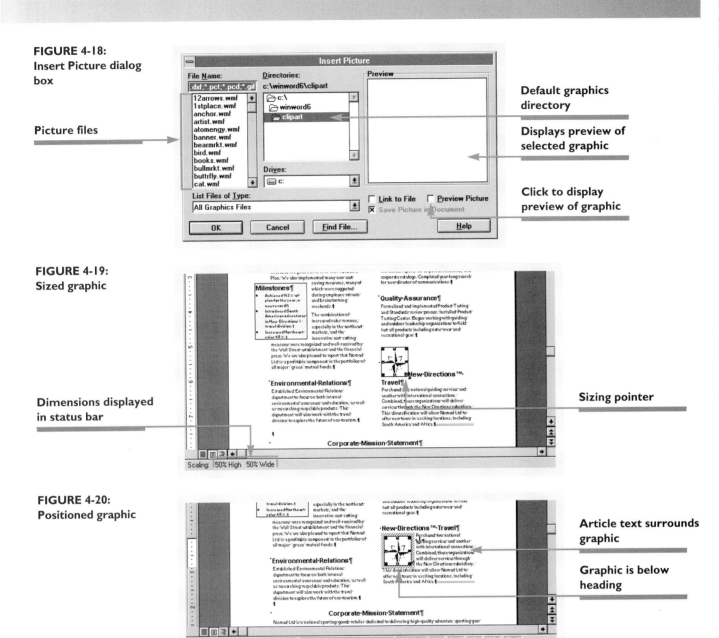

FIGURE 4-20:
Positioned graphic

Article text surrounds graphic

Graphic is below heading

FIGURE 4-21:
Completed document

Inserted graphics

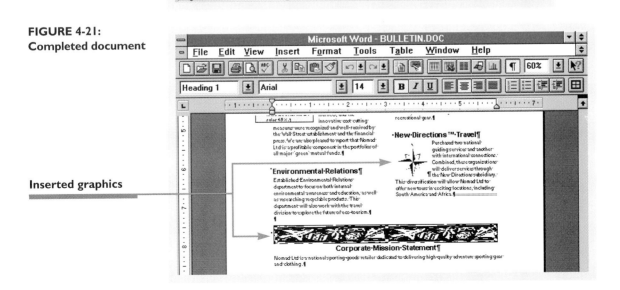

Creating headers and footers

Information that appears at the top of every page in a document is called a **header**; information that appears at the bottom of every page in a document is called a **footer**. Headers and footers usually contain basic information such as the page number, the date, or the document name. In Word you can type the text you want to appear in headers and footers, or you can insert fields to supply specific information automatically. ▶ As a finishing touch to the *Executive Bulletin*, Angela wants to include the date and the volume and issue number in the header. In the footer, she will include the company name and a copyright symbol.

1 Click **View** on the menu bar, then click **Header and Footer**
The Header and Footer toolbar appears, as shown in Figure 4-22. The text in the body of the document appears grayed out; you cannot edit the text of the document when you display the Header and Footer toolbar. The header area of the document is outlined with a dashed rectangle, which does not appear when you print the document. In the header area, Angela types the volume and issue number of the bulletin.

2 With the insertion point in the Header-Section 1 area, type **Volume 1, Issue 1**
The text appears in the header. Next, Angela includes the date at the right margin.

3 Press **[Tab]** twice then click the **Date button** 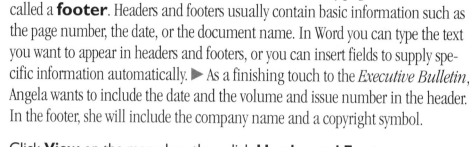 on the Header and Footer toolbar
Your computer's system date appears at the right margin. Now, Angela wants to add a footer at the bottom of the page.

4 Click the **Switch Between Header and Footer button** 📘 on the Header and Footer toolbar to move to the footer area
The Footer-Section 1 area appears in the document window. Angela can now enter the copyright information she wants to include as part of the bulletin. First, she inserts the copyright symbol.

5 Click **Insert** on the menu bar, then click **Symbol**
The Symbol dialog box opens, as shown in Figure 4-23. Depending on the fonts available on your computer, your Symbol dialog box might look different. Make sure that either the Symbol or [normal text] font appears in the Font list box (click the Font list arrow to select one of these fonts, if necessary). Angela locates the copyright symbol (©) and inserts it in the footer.

6 Click **©**, click **Insert**, then click **Close**
The copyright symbol appears in the footer. Angela can continue typing the rest of the text for the copyright notice.

7 Type **1995, Nomad Ltd** then click the **Close button** on the Header and Footer toolbar
The document now contains text in the header and footer.

8 Click the **Print Preview button** 🔍 on the Standard toolbar to see how the document will look when printed, then click the **Print button** 🖨 on the Print Preview toolbar
Compare your printed document to Figure 4-24.

9 Click the **Save button** 💾 on the Standard toolbar, click **File** on the menu bar, then click **Exit**

FIGURE 4-22: Viewing the header

Header area

Header and Footer
toolbar

Switch Between
Header and Footer
button

Date button

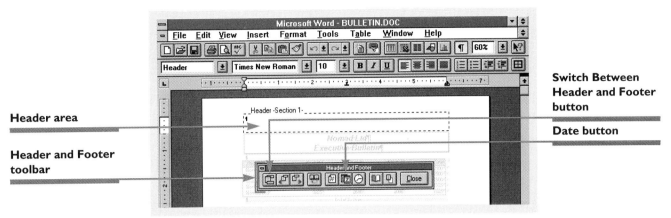

FIGURE 4-23: Symbol dialog box

Choose either Symbol
or [normal text] font

Copyright symbol

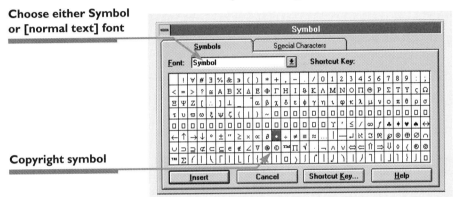

FIGURE 4-24:
Completed document

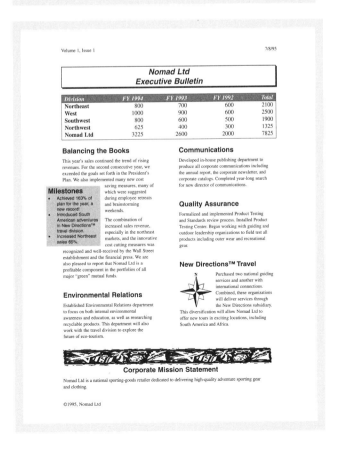

CONCEPTSREVIEW

Label each item of the newsletter shown in Figure 4-25.

1 _____

2 _____

3 _____

4 _____

5 _____

6 _____

7 _____

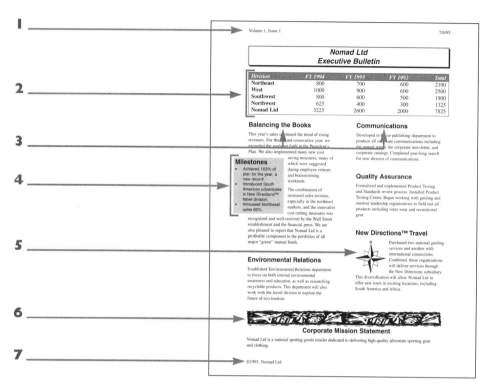

FIGURE 4-25

Match each of the following terms with the statement that best describes its function.

8 Table

9 Gridlines

10 Cell

11 SUM

12 Frame

13 Section

14 Sizing handles

15 Column break

16 Header

17 Columns button

a. Allow you to size an object

b. Arranges text in rows and columns

c. Separates each intersection of rows and columns in a table

d. Allows you to position text or graphics anywhere on the page

e. The intersection of a row and column in a table

f. Allows you to format individual parts of a document with different settings

g. The default calculation with the Formula command

h. Moves text from one column to the next

i. Formats text into columns using default settings

j. Text at the top of every page

Select the best answer from the list of choices.

18 To insert a column at the end of a table, you must first

   a. Select the last column

   b. Place the insertion point in the last column

   c. Select the last cell in the table

   d. Select the end-of-row markers at the right edge of the table

19 Before positioning text or a graphic without changing the formatting of surrounding text, you must first

   a. Select the object and size it

   b. Select the object and insert a frame

   c. Select the object and move it

   d. Select the object then click the Frame button

20 To insert a header you click View, click Header and Footer, and then

   a. Click the Header check box, and type the text of the header

   b. Click the Go to Top button, and type the text of the header

   c. Type the text of the header

   d. Enter your header preferences and text in the Insert Header dialog box

APPLICATIONSREVIEW

1 Create a table.

a. Start Word.

b. Open the document named UNIT_4-2.DOC from your Student Disk and save it as SQUARPEG.DOC to your MY_FILES directory.

c. With the insertion point in front of the paragraph mark above the heading Othello, click the Insert Table button on the Standard toolbar and drag to select a grid that is four columns wide and five rows long.

d. Enter price information in the table, using Figure 4-26:

2 Format the table.

a. With the insertion point inside the table, click Table then click Table AutoFormat.

b. Be sure the AutoFit and Last Column check boxes are cleared, and that the Last Row check box is checked.

c. Choose the Simple 1 format and click OK.

d. Select the first row of the table.

e. Click the Borders button on the Formatting toolbar, then click the Shading list arrow on the Borders toolbar and choose 5% shading.

f. Click the Borders button on the Formatting toolbar to hide the Borders toolbar.

3 Use columns to format text.

a. Click outside of the table, click the Columns button on the Standard toolbar, then drag to select three columns.

b. Click the Page Layout View button on the horizontal scroll bar.

c. Place the insertion point in front of the heading Macbeth. Click Insert, click Break, click the Column Break radio button, then click OK.

d. Place the insertion point in front of the heading Hamlet, then press [F4] and save your work.

4 Create and format sections.

a. Place the insertion point in front of the heading Othello. Click Insert, click Break, click the Continuous radio button, then click OK.

b. Place the insertion point in section 1, click the Columns button on the Standard toolbar, then click one column.

c. Place the insertion point before the paragraph mark above the heading Still Can't Decide?, click Insert, click Break, click the Continuous radio button, then click OK.

d. Click the Columns button on the Standard toolbar, then click one column and save your work.

5 Position text and graphics using frames.

a. Select the chart object near the end of the document.

b. Drag the bottom-left corner sizing handle up and to the right until the chart is 90% of its original height and 90% of its original width.

c. Click Insert then click Frame.

d. Drag the chart to the left of the last paragraph on the previous page, aligning the anchor icon with the first bullet item and the left edge of the chart with the left margin.

e. Select the entire shaded paragraph near the beginning of the document, click Insert, then click Frame.

f. Drag the right center sizing handle to the left until the frame is about 1" wide.

g. Position the pointer over a border of the frame until the pointer changes to the frame pointer, then drag the framed text 1½" to the left and ½" down.

h. Click the Center button on the Formatting toolbar, then save your work.

6 Insert graphics.

a. Place the insertion point before the paragraph mark above the heading Still Can't Decide?, click Insert, then click Picture.

b. In the File Name list box click DIVIDER3.WMF, then click the Preview Picture check box (if it is not already selected) and click OK.

c. Select the graphic (if it is not already selected), then drag the right center sizing handle to the right margin.

d. Drag the bottom center sizing handle down about ½" then save your work.

7 Insert headers and footers.

a. Click View then click Header and Footer.

b. Type "Winter 1995" in the header area.

c. Click the Switch Between Header and Footer button on the Header and Footer toolbar.

d. Click Insert then click Symbol.

e. Click ©, click Insert, then click Close.

f. Type "1995, Square Peg Theatre."

g. Click the Close button on the Header and Footer toolbar.

h. Preview, then print the document and compare it to Figure 4-26.

i. Close the file, then exit Word.

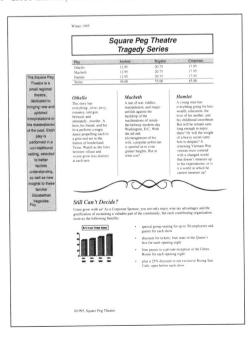

FIGURE 4-26

INDEPENDENT
CHALLENGE 1

As the marketing manager of a large computer company, you are responsible for producing an executive summary to the corporate report. Using the document in Figure 4-27 as a guide, create a document that identifies the highlights of the past year. To save time, you can start with a draft named UNIT_4-3.DOC from your Student Disk and save it as BIGSYS.DOC to your MY_FILES directory.

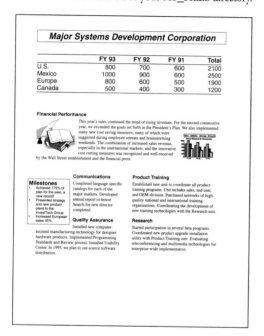

FIGURE 4-27

INDEPENDENT
CHALLENGE 2

Nomad Ltd would like its shareholders who want to attend the Annual Meeting to complete a short registration form. Format the table, and use frames and the CLIPART file called PARTY.WMF to create a registration form that looks like the one shown in Figure 4-28. Start by opening the draft document named UNIT_4-4.DOC from your Student Disk and save it as INVITE.DOC to your MY_FILES directory.

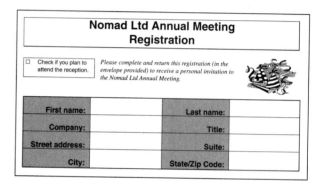

FIGURE 4-28

Glossary

Alignment   The horizontal position of text within the width of a line or between tab stops.

Application   A software program, such as Microsoft Word.

Application window   A window that contains the running application. It displays the menus and provides the workspace for any document used within the application.

Arrow keys   The [↑], [↓], [←], and [→] keys. Used to move the insertion point or to select menu commands or options.

Automatic save   A feature that automatically saves document changes in a temporary file at specified intervals.

AutoCorrect   A feature that automatically corrects a misspelled word that you type. Word provides several entries for commonly misspelled words, but you can add your own.

AutoFormat   A feature that improves the appearance of a document by applying consistent formatting and styles based on a default document template or a document template you select.

AutoText entry   A stored text or graphic you want to use again.

Border   A straight vertical or horizontal line between columns in a section, next to or around paragraphs and graphics, or in a table. *See also* Rule.

Bullet   A small graphic, usually a round or square dot, often used to identify items in a list.

Cell   The intersection of a row and a column.

Cell reference   The address or name of a specific cell. Each cell reference contains a letter (A, B, C, and so on) to identify its column and a number (1, 2, 3, and so on) to identify its row.

Character style   A stored set of text format settings.

Click   To press and release a mouse button in one motion.

Clipboard   A temporary storage area for cut or copied text or graphics. You can paste the contents of the Clipboard into any Word document. The Clipboard holds the information until you cut or copy another piece of text or a graphic.

Control menu   A menu that includes commands with which you can control the size and position of the Word window and switch to another application.

Crop   To cut away the parts of a graphic you don't want to appear.

Cut   A command that removes selected text or a graphic from a document and places it on the Clipboard so you can paste it to another place in the document or to another document.

Default template   A template with the file name NORMAL.DOT that contains default menus, AutoCorrect entries, styles, and page setup settings. Documents use the global template unless you specify a custom template. *See also* Template.

Defaults   Predefined settings such as page margins, tab spacing, and shortcut key assignments. The default template when you create documents is NORMAL.DOT.

Dialog box   A windows that appears when you choose a command whose name is followed by an ellipsis (...). A dialog box allows you to make selections that determine how the command affects the selected area.

Directories   Subdivisions of a disk that work like a filing system to help you organize files.

Document window   A rectangular portion of the screen in which you view and edit a document. You can have up to nine document windows open in the Word application window.

Drag   To hold down the mouse button while moving the mouse.

Drive   A mechanism in a computer or an area on a network used to retrieve and store information. Personal computers often have one hard disk drive labeled C and two drives labeled A and B that read removable floppy disks.

Edit   To add, delete, or change text and graphics.

Effects   Refers to whether text appears in small caps, all caps, hidden text, struckthrough, subscripted, or superscripted.

Extend selection   To lengthen a selection. When you extend a selection, it grows progressively larger each time you press [F8]. To shrink the selection, press [Shift] + [F8].

File   A document that has been created, then saved, under a unique file name.

Font   A name given to a collection of characters (letters, numerals, symbols, and punctuation marks) with a specific design. Arial and Times New Roman are examples of font names.

Font size   Refers to the physical size of text, measured in points (pts). One inch equals 72 points.

Font style   Refers to whether text appears as bold, italicized, or underlined, or any combination of these formats.

Format   The way text appears on a page. In Word, a format comes from direct formatting and the application of styles. The four types of formats are character, paragraph, section, and document.

Formatting toolbar   A bar that contains buttons and options for the most frequently used Word formatting commands.

Frame   A box you add to mark an area of text or graphic in a document so that you can easily position it on a page. Once you insert an object into a frame, you can drag it to the position you want in page layout view.

Graphics   A picture, chart, or drawing in a document.

Graphic object   An element in a document that can be moved, sized, and modified without leaving Word.

Hanging indent   A paragraph format in which the first line of a paragraph starts farther left than the subsequent lines.

Header and footer   A header is text or graphics that appear at the top of every page in a section. A footer appears at the bottom of every page. Headers and footers often contain page numbers, chapter titles, dates, and author names. Headers and footers appear in the header or footer pane for editing.

Hidden text   A character format that allows you to show or hide designated text. Word indicates hidden text by underlining it with a dotted line.

Horizontal ruler   A graphical bar displayed across the top of the document window in all views. You can use the ruler to indent paragraphs, set tab stops, adjust left and right paragraph margins, and change column widths in a table.

Indent   The distance between text boundaries and page margins.

Insertion point   Blinking vertical line on the Word screen that shows your current location and where text and graphics are inserted.

Landscape   A term used to refer to horizontal page orientation; opposite of portrait, or vertical, orientation.

Line break   Mark inserted where you want to end one line and start another without starting a new paragraph.

Line spacing   The height of a line of text, including extra spacing. Line spacing is often measured in lines or points.

Margin   The distance between the edge of the text in the document and the top, bottom, or side edges of the page.

Menu bar   The horizontal bar under the title bar that lists the names of the menus that contain Word commands.

Nonprinting characters   Marks displayed on the screen to indicate characters that do not print, such as tab characters or paragraph marks.

Normal view   The view you see when you start Word. Normal view is used for most editing and formatting tasks.

Object   A table, chart, graphic, equation, or other form of information you create and edit with an application other than Word, but whose data you insert and store in a Word document.

Overtype   An option for replacing existing characters one by one as you type. When you select the Overtype option, the letters "OVR" appear in the status bar.

Page break   The point at which one page ends and another begins. A break you insert (created by pressing [Ctrl] + [Enter]) is called a hard break; a break determined by the page layout is called a soft break.

Page layout view   A view of a document as it will appear when you print it.

Paragraph style   A stored set of paragraph format settings.

Paste   To insert cut or copied text into a document from the temporary storage area called the Clipboard.

Point size   A measurement used for the size of text characters. There are 72 points per inch.

Portrait   A term used to refer to vertical page orientation; opposite of "landscape," or horizontal, orientation.

Record   The entire collection of fields related to an item or individual, contained in the data source.

Repaginate   To calculate and insert page breaks at the correct point in a document.

Repetitive text   Text that you use often in documents.

Rule   A straight vertical or horizontal line between columns in a section, next to paragraphs, or in a table. You can assign a variety of widths to a rule. *See also* Border.

Sans serif font   A font whose characters do not include serifs, the small strokes at the ends of the characters. Arial is a sans serif font.

Scale   To change the height and/or width of a graphic by a percentage. You can choose to preserve or change the relative proportions of elements within the graphic.

Scroll bars   Bars that appear on the right and bottom borders of a window that allow you to scroll the window vertically and horizontally to view portions of the document not currently visible.

Selection bar   An unmarked column at the left edge of a document window used to select text with the mouse.

Serif font   A font that has small strokes at the ends of the characters. Times New Roman and Palatino are serif fonts.

Shading   The color or pattern behind text or graphics.

Soft return   A line break created by pressing [Shift] + [Enter]. This creates a new line without creating a new paragraph.

Standard toolbar   The topmost bar of buttons that provides access to frequently used Word commands.

Status bar   The horizontal bar located at the bottom of the Word window. It displays the current page number and section number, the total number of pages in the document, and the vertical position (in inches) of the insertion point. You also see the status of commands in effect, and the current time, as well as descriptions of commands and buttons as you move around the window.

Style   A group of formatting instructions that you name and store and are able to modify. When you apply a style to selected characters and paragraphs, all the formatting instructions of that style are applied at once.

Style area   An area to the left of the selection in which the names of applied styles are displayed.

Style Gallery   A feature that allows you to examine the overall formatting and styles used in a document template. With the Style Gallery you can also preview your document formatted in the styles from a selected template.

Tab stop   A measured position for placing and aligning text at a specific place on a line. Word has four kinds of tab stops, left-aligned (the default), centered, right-aligned, and decimal.

Table   One or more rows of cells commonly used to display numbers and other items for quick reference and analysis. Items in a table are organized into rows and columns. You can convert text into a table with the Insert Table command on the Table menu.

Template   A special kind of document that provides basic tools and text for creating a document. Templates can contain the following elements: styles, AutoText items, macros, customized menu and key assignments, and text or graphics that are the same in different types of documents.

Title bar   The horizontal bar at the top of a window that displays the name of the document or application that appears in that window. Until you save the document and give it a name, the temporary name for the document is DOCUMENT1.

Toolbar   A horizontal bar with buttons that provide access to the most commonly used commands in Word, such as opening, copying, and printing files.

ToolTip   When you move the pointer over a button, the name of the button appears below the button and a brief description of its function appears in the status bar.

Vertical alignment   The placement of text on a page in relation to the top, bottom, or center of the page.

Vertical ruler   A graphical bar displayed at the left edge of the document window in the page layout and print preview views. You can use this ruler to adjust the top and bottom page margins, and change row height in a table.

View   A display that shows certain aspects of the document. Word has six views: normal, draft, outline, page layout, full screen, and print preview.

View buttons   Appear in the horizontal scroll bar. Allow you to display the document in one of three views: Normal, Page Layout, and Outline.

Wizard   A feature that provides a series of dialog boxes that guide you through the process of creating a specific document.

Word processing application   An application used for creating documents efficiently. Usually includes features beyond simple editing, such as formatting and arranging text and graphics to create attractive documents, as well as the ability to merge documents for form letters and envelopes.

Word-wrap   Automatic placement of a word on the next line. When you type text and reach the right margin or indent, Word checks to see if the entire word you type fits on the current line. If not, Word automatically places the entire word on the next line.

WYSIWYG (What You See Is What You Get)   An application that indicates a document will print with the same formatting that is displayed in the document window.

Index